# Maynard 8 Miles

A Story of Family, Basketball and Triumph in the Heartland.
The Legacy of Carolyn Nicholson and Glenn Borland

As told by: Brian J. Borland

## FOREWORD
*By former Wisconsin Governor Jim Doyle*

I love small town Midwestern life. I love basketball. And I love the story of Glenn and Carolyn Borland, lovingly researched and told by their son, Brian.

As a young boy I sat in the far reaches of the upper deck of the old University of Wisconsin Fieldhouse and watched a blond Iowan, playing for the Badgers, raining left-handed hook shots down from all points on the court. Say the words "left-handed hook shot" to any Wisconsin basketball junkie of my vintage, and he or she will say "Glenn Borland." I was lucky enough several years later to have him as my first basketball coach at Madison West Junior High School. When I was a senior and a starter on the West High team, Glenn Borland and his hook shot singlehandedly beat us in the faculty-varsity game. But despite all his accomplishments, he was only the second-best basketball player in the family.

While we all knew about Glenn's accomplishments in Wisconsin, we only had a sort of dim awareness that Carolyn had done something remarkable. This was because of Carolyn's modesty. In this book, through Brian's painstaking research, we learn that Carolyn Borland's story is the stuff of legend. In Wisconsin, as in most states at the time, high school girls did not play competitive sports. Yet just across the Mississippi River in Iowa things were different. Six-on-six girls' basketball was huge, and Carolyn Borland was its biggest star. Much of this book is her story, a story of a farm girl who through natural gifts, hard work, perseverance and incredible poise under pressure led her small town team to the state championship before 15,000 people and a statewide audience.

It is also a story of a young woman who paved the way for so many more to come. "Girls should not play competitive sports," they said in the first two thirds of the twentieth century. Carolyn Borland and all the young women who played Iowa Girls'

Basketball proved them wrong. While we regret that their great version of the game has disappeared, think how great Carolyn, and her 5'11" sister, Glenda, would have been playing full court five-on-five. And think about the millions of young women across this country playing all kinds of sports today. When I read this book, I think of my young granddaughters and all the choices they will have, and I say "Thank you, Carolyn."

Maynard and Oelwein, Iowa and basketball, of course, were not the end, but just the start of the lives of Glenn and Carolyn Borland. Glenn, with Carolyn at his side, went on to become a great educator. Thousands of young people in Madison, including my sons, were enriched by his career as a teacher, coach, principal and administrator. I am often asked what it takes to have a strong school system and I answer that it takes people like Glenn Borland. Respect and honor teachers. Care about every student who walks through the door. Deal honestly and directly with people. Adhere to time –honored values, but understand that times are changing. The boy with a left-handed hook shot, and the girl with a silky smooth head fake and drive took all they learned in those small Iowa towns and went on to lead lives of caring and service. This is the story they were too modest to tell. I hope you enjoy it as much as I did.

# DEDICATION

*Maynard 8 Miles is dedicated to my Mother, Carolyn Nicholson Borland, and to my Father, Glenn F. Borland, the two most humble people in the world. This is also dedicated to the Borland and Nicholson families and to anyone who dares to dream.*

# ACKNOWLEDGEMENTS

I would first like to thank Elaine Lohr. You gave me confidence early on to keep the story alive.

I would also like to acknowledge the Maynard 8 Miles focus group. You all played a major role in helping me create the book:

Rob Aubey, Nathan Brinkman, Scott and Stephanie Barth, Kay Coombs, John and Sarah DiVall, Todd Green, Fred Hable, Tom and Lisa Kermgard, Kent Fitch, Mike Miller, Tim Nybroten, Tim and Kim Pederson, Dean Statz, Dave and Patti Richardson Nancy Schuman, Reno Simonini, Steve Williams, and Bob and Sandy Richards. A special thank you to Cass Comerford and Adam Burton of Capra Strategies for making my dream come true.

Thanks to Pat Reardon, a true professional who always believed in me.

To my dad and my Aunt Glenda, thanks so much for your love and encouragement. We all wish mom was here to see this. And of course my brother Brad and sister Liz and my children, Brianna, Alex and Brooke for all your patience during the past five years.

Lastly and most importantly, my lovely wife Char. I could not have completed this book without your love and encouragement.

Mom, we did it!!

### A NOTE TO THE READER:

I have spent a number of years researching the historical background of my mom and dad's basketball experience and their relationship. The historical context of the book was based on my investigation and is set forth to the best of my knowledge.

# TABLE OF CONTENTS

# INTRODUCTION

To the casual traveler, the roads between Madison, Wisconsin, and northeastern Iowa may not seem to be anything special. But to me, those roads, with their pastoral scenes and familiar landmarks, are part of the fabric of my life, part of who I am, and part of who my family is.

On a snowy day in 2005, about a year after my beloved Grandma Ruth Nicholson died at age 95, I was driving from Des Moines, Iowa, to Madison, Wisconsin. I passed a sign that said "Highway 3." I sure do know Highway 3. It leads to Maynard, the tiny town in Iowa where my mother grew up. But Grandma Ruth had been my last tie to Maynard. I didn't turn onto Highway 3 that day, but as I passed that sign I felt a pang.

The previous year, along with my brother Brad, who lives in Los Angeles, I drove from Madison to Maynard because we had been alerted that Grandma Ruth wasn't faring well. When we walked into her room, we were devastated to see her fading away, dying. We remembered our grandma full of energy and laughter, a hardy farm wife, the mother of five kids, grandmother of fifteen, and the great grandmother to dozens.

Just eleven months before, vigorous and healthy at age 94, she had made the trip from Maynard to Madison to see my children, Brianna, Alex and Brooke. She would be meeting Brooke, her youngest great-grandchild, for the first time. But now, only a year later, she was in obvious pain and was moaning that her legs hurt. She could barely open her eyes, her beautiful face was pale, and her outgoing smile was gone.

Brad and I went up to Grandma Ruth, and I said, "It's Brad and Brian; it's Brad and Brian." She slightly opened one eye and said, "Boys, boys." We said we loved her and missed her. All she said was, "Hold my hands, hold my hands." So we held, hugged, squeezed, and kissed those precious 95-year-old hands.

A little later, as we left the room, she called for us: "Where are the boys? Where are the boys?" We went back in the room. And when we eventually told her we were leaving, she sat up and clearly blurted out, "You boys drive home safe." She knew, somehow, that we were going back to Madison, as I had been doing for 41 years. As we left, we knew that we wouldn't see her again. Two days later, she passed away.

So as I passed Highway 3 a year later on my way from Des Moines to Madison, I was suddenly hit by the poignant realization that I might never go to Maynard again.

It was those thoughts of my Grandma Ruth combined with the special feeling I got traveling those roads that inspired me to write this book, which tells a story of life, death, love, hardship, triumph and basketball.

Grandma Ruth at the age of 94 made the trip to Madison to meet her youngest great granddaughter Brooke.
Pictured:Top Row: Glenn Borland, Liz Borland,Carolyn Borland
Middle Row: Brianna Borland, Brian Borland, Brooke Borland, Grandma Ruth
Front Row: Char Borland, Alex Borland

The entrance to Maynard High School.

A picture of the Nicholson farm. This picture was taken in 1941 shortly after Glenn and Ruth purchased the farm.

Ruth Holmstrom  6-16-29
21 years old

My future grandmother, Ruth Holmstrom at age 21 in 1929. She was a real Swedish-American beauty.

Ruth Nicholson's mother Louisa Carlson, my great grandmother, would be a passenger on the ship Aurania and arrive in the United States on April 25, 1892, from Sweden. Sixteen years later in 1908 she would give birth to Ruth Holmstrom.

A young Glenn Nicholson around the time he would be introduced to Ruth Holmstrom.

## CHAPTER 1
## A DECISION CHANGES THE GIRLS' LIVES

Shortly after World War II ended, my grandfather, Glenn Nicholson, made a decision that would have a considerable impact on girls' basketball in Iowa.

In the early 1930s, Glenn had been playing on a semi-pro baseball team with a young Swede named Oscar Holmstrom. He had a sister named Ruth, a breathtakingly beautiful young woman. At age 16, she was working as a waitress. Glenn and Ruth met, quickly decided that they were meant for each other, and in 1932 they were married. They accepted an offer of $50 to hold their wedding in the grandstand at the Buchanan County fair in front of what the Bulletin Journal called on Thursday September 15th "a huge crowd." Fifty dollars was a lot of money in those early days of the Depression, and Ruth spent part of that $50 on a cook stove, which fed the family that grew to seven over the next seven years as the couple had four daughters and one son in that time.

Their third daughter, Carolyn, my mother, was born in 1937.

In 1941, Glenn and Ruth bought a 240 acre farm and settled into a life of successful farming. They raised beef cattle and hogs, and they planted beans, oats, and corn. The farm was three miles outside of Maynard, a town of fewer than 500 people in the northeastern quadrant of the state.

In 1946 Glenn Nicholson made his historic decision, which ultimately put Maynard on the map. Having played baseball himself, he believed his kids should have a sport, and he felt that the sport should be basketball. Basketball was very popular among girls throughout the state, even though the high school they would eventually attend didn't have a girls' basketball team.

He determined that his kids should have a basketball hoop and backboard. In those days, when you lived on an Iowa farm you didn't go out and buy a basket; you made one. So, although Glenn probably bought a rim, he built the rest himself. Glenn and the kids decided to put the basket in the hayloft, the "upstairs" of the barn, so to get to their new basketball court, the kids would have to climb the ladder to the loft. The hayloft was perfect for winter, but in summer hay had to be stored in the loft, so every spring Glenn would take the basket out of the loft and bolt it to the garage, and the Nicholson kids were able to play basketball year-round.

When the basket made its first appearance in the Nicholson barn, my mother Carolyn was 8, and her younger sister Glenda was 7. Lou Ann was the oldest at 13, Betty was 11 and the youngest, Jim, was 5. The kids immediately took to their new basketball court, especially the girls.

These were farm girls, and like farm girls everywhere, they had to help with the chores. At 5 each morning, Ruth would shout up to them that it was time to get up. Sometimes the girls would just turn over and pull the blankets tighter. Then Glenn would bellow the same message, and all four girls would bolt out of their beds. The chores included lifting and dragging heavy bushel baskets full of grain to feed the cattle. Glenn was an excellent farmer with exacting standards. He insisted not only that each job be done well, but he also wanted the farm to always look good. He was a stern disciplinarian, and he oversaw the girls' chores like a first sergeant.

With the chores done, the girls would get ready for school. Academics were very important in the Nicholson household. Glenn Nicholson was a kind and fair man, but also very strict. He instilled a strong work ethic in his children that encompassed school, farm work and basketball. With his connections in the Maynard school system, academics took on a special focus in the Nicholson children's lives and played a key role in the formation of their identities.

After school, with their farm chores and their school homework done, the girls still found hours each day for basketball. On non-school-days, they put in basketball marathons. And in that barn they played hard. They played H-O-R-S-E, they did shoot-arounds, and they played vigorous one-on-one and two-on-two games. The two-on-two games usually involved the younger girls, Carolyn and Glenda, playing against the two older girls. The older girls never showed any mercy; they would always win, and then they'd rub it in with some trash talk. Betty's taunts were particularly sharp. She would tell the two younger girls that "You're no good, and you'll never be any good." All of this helped make Carolyn and Glenda super-competitive. It also made them better players.

Anyone who plays long and hard at something tends to get good at it. And month after month, year after year, the girls were building an impressive set of basketball skills. They were becoming deadly shooters, crisp passers, and smooth ball handlers. Although they didn't realize it at the time, playing against each other gave them some of the toughest competition they would ever face on a basketball court.

Carolyn and Glenda took to listening to radio broadcasts of the Iowa Girls' State Basketball Tournament. They had been told about Maynard not having a girls' team, and that concerned them, even at a young age. Even so, the two of them carved a message on their bedroom wall when they were aged 8 and 9 that reflected their dream to play in the Iowa girls' state tournament. Their carving said; "Maynard State Champs 1956."

Unfortunately, the likelihood of winning a state championship when you don't have a team is nil. The Nicholson girls had been told that Maynard wasn't big enough to support a team, and that the school district did not have enough money for a girls' program. That didn't make any sense to the girls. Most of the other small towns in Iowa had a girls' team. In the 1950s it was estimated that 70% of high school girls played basketball. Why not Maynard?

Ruth Nicholson told the girls the real reason Maynard did not have a team. In the 1920s Maynard had a very good girls' team. They made it to the state tournament in 1924, and in 1926 Maynard's star Irene Silka scored 110 points in one game. At some point after the 1926 season one of the girls on the Maynard team died while playing in a game. Her death was wrongly blamed on her playing basketball. The Maynard School Board immediately discontinued all girls' sports (basketball was really the only girls' sport) and sided with popular national sentiment at the time, which said that girls should not be playing high school sports. That sports suspension by the Maynard School

Board was temporary.

Later in 1926, Maynard re-instated girls' basketball. The Maynard team, however, was never able to build on the success of the 1924-1926 teams, and the team's record for the next fifteen or so years was unimpressive.

In 1943 Maynard officially canceled girls' basketball. Because of World War II, resources were very limited, including gas for driving to and from towns for games. The other reason that was cited was lack of interest. Not many girls were turning out to play, and as the war went on, most families and potential players lost any interest in basketball. There was no uproar over the cancellation of the girls' program. People had other things on their minds. As it was in countries all over the world, the war took its toll on Iowa. One shock to the people of the state was the fact that five brothers from one Iowa family, the Sullivan family of Waterloo, were killed when the light cruiser they all served on was sunk.

In 1949 Glenn Nicholson was elected to the Maynard School Board. The girls felt they now had an advocate in a good position to make a team happen. They begged him to do whatever he could to get Maynard a girls' basketball team. So Glenn pitched the idea to the board, and his fellow members of the board turned him down. The board members said the girls' safety and lack of money were not the reasons this time. They said Maynard simply did not have enough players to make a girls' team viable.

The Nicholson girls were devastated, and their tears were flowing. They would not be able to compete with others in the game they had come to love. Furthermore, they had developed an extraordinary amount of basketball ability, and they would have nowhere to showcase it.

But the next year, 1950, with the girls' basketball future looking most bleak, fate intervened. The Fish family came to town.

The proud Nicholson family in 1942.
From left: Glenn, Glenda, Lou Ann, Betty, Jim, Ruth and Carolyn.

A picture of the future basketball stars. Carolyn, 9, on the left and Glenda, 8. This is the age when they developed their love for playing basketball.

A more recent picture of the Nicholson farm, a beautiful place to visit.

With the farmhouse in the background, this is a picture of the Nicholson kids about the age they started playing basketball in the hayloft.From Left: Carolyn 7 1/2, Betty 9 1/2, Lou Ann 11, Glenda 6 and Jim 4.

## Gem A: PORTRAIT OF THE TOWN

Like many an Iowa town, Maynard's environs are full of hogs, corn, and Lutherans. But Maynard was a place without any claim to fame.

Small towns in Iowa have produced some well-known people. John Wayne was from Winterset, Iowa. Artist Grant Wood, best known for his painting of an Iowa farm couple that was variously called "American Gothic" or "The Iowa Farmers," was born in Anamosa, Iowa, and lived for a while in Cedar Rapids. Herbert Hoover was born and reared in West Branch, Iowa, and later spent some time in Washington, D.C. But he had no known connection to Maynard. Bob Feller, the hard throwing Hall of Fame pitcher for the Cleveland Indians, spent much of his youth pitching baseballs at the side of the family barn. But that barn was in Van Meter, Iowa, which is quite a ways from Maynard. Meredith Willson wrote a popular musical, "The Music Man," about life in a small Iowa town. He set it in fictional River City, which was modeled not after Maynard, but after his native Mason City. So fame has eluded Maynard.

Similarly, historic events tended not to have happened in Maynard. No major battles were fought there, and no life-changing inventions were made there. John Dillinger, the James gang, and Bonnie and Clyde robbed banks all over the Midwest and the Great Plains, but none of them ever pulled a job in Maynard. So while it had always been a place where hard-working, decent heartland people lived out there lives, Maynard did not have spotlights shining on it.

In addition to not being in the spotlight, Maynard wasn't big enough to have a stoplight. Main Street was only about a block long, and the town had the bare essentials of what constituted a town: a gas station, a diner, a couple of bars, a bank, a school, and a nice park. The Volga River, one of the very few rivers in North America that flows from south to north, runs through the town.

*Brian Borland*

My dad with my grandmother, whom I never had the honor of meeting.

My dad with my grandfather, who died when I was 4 years old.

Linda takes young Glenn to visit his father at one of the wreckage sites.

## CHAPTER 2
## 'YOU ARE MY ONLY PARENTS!'

Oelwein, Iowa, is eight miles south of Maynard. Oelwein is the biggest town in Iowa's Fayette County, and it's where Maynard people go to do their shopping and a lot of their other business. These days it has a population of about 6,400.

While Carolyn Nicholson, who would become my mother, was shooting baskets in the hayloft of the family barn, in Maynard, Iowa, the boy who would become my father was cutting his basketball teeth in a garage in Oelwein.

My dad had been adopted at the age of 3 months. I always wonder about his birth parents, who they were and why they gave my dad up. Our family is not sure where he was born, but we think we know what his name at birth was. He was adopted from the Lutheran Orphans Home in Waverly, Iowa. His adoptive parents were Glenn and Linda Borland. His adopted name would be Glenn Frederick Borland.

Glenn Borland Sr. was a foreman on the railroad in Oelwein, which was a railroad hub in the 1930s, '40s, and '50s. He was head of the wrecking crew in charge of removing damaged railroad cars. Glenn would be on call 24 hours a day, 365 days a year to coordinate relief efforts at crash sites and to operate the cranes to remove the damaged cars. Today in downtown Oelwein sits a railroad museum, and on display is a picture of Glenn Borland Sr. honoring him for his hard work keeping railroad passengers safe as they traveled through Iowa.

Glenn and Linda could not have children of their own. I've always wondered why they waited so long to adopt, as they were 40 years old when they adopted their first and only child. How excited they must have been after having waited so long. My Grandma Linda died before I was born, and Glenn Borland Sr. died when I was 4. I don't remember Grandpa Borland, but I do have some pictures of us together that I will always cherish.

Glenn Sr., Linda and young Glenn lived in a very small house in Oelwein; two bedrooms, a kitchen, one bathroom and a small living room. Glenn Sr. bought the house from a man who had a business painting cars, so behind the tiny house was a nine-car garage. The Borlands turned the garage into a indoor basketball court and for baskets they used peach baskets. All of the kids in the neighborhood were invited over to play.

The kids shared the garage with the Borland family pet, a horse named Babe. Babe was a hit with neighborhood kids. Little Glenn would hitch Babe up to a buggy and would charge other kids 10 cents for a buggy ride around the neighborhood. They also had a family dog, Spike. Glenn, Linda, little Glenn, Babe and Spike were a close and happy family. When little Glenn was still very young, Glenn Sr. and Linda came to realize that the boy they had adopted at age 3 months was not only an interesting and special kid, he was also an exceptional athlete. Despite not being athletes themselves, the Borlands recognized that Glenn Jr. was ahead of other boys his age physically. All he ever wanted to do was play sports, and whenever he did play, Glenn Jr. excelled.

Back in 1936 when Glenn and Linda adopted my dad there was another 3-month-old boy in Waverly in the same adoption agency. That little boy turned out to be Bob Richards, who was adopted one week after Glenn. Coincidentally, both sets of adoptive parents lived in Oelwein. They had never met and had no idea they each were adopting a boy. Glenn and Bob met each other at age 4, and were always together as they grew up. They both had a love of sports and family. The two continue to be best friends to this day. Bob, who retired after a career as a John Deere dealer and then as a Deere executive, lives in Arizona, and Glenn lives in Madison, and they make it a point to get together two or three times a year.

Amazingly, it wasn't until years later that the adoptive parents of Glenn and Bob learned that they had adopted the boys from the same agency at about the same time. They pieced the situation together while conversing at an event at the boys' middle school.

In Glenn's 1954 yearbook, Bob wrote to his best friend: "Studly Borland, pretty soon all the kids that we grew up with will be gone and we won't ever see them again. I know one thing that you and I will always be together. I don't care if you are on one side of the 48 states and I'm on the other. You're a great basketball player, Glenn. You should have a very great career. Some time when things go wrong just think, you are really a good player, like I always did, it will help you. - Bob"

When I came across and read that note that Bob had written to Glenn a half century ago, it occurred to me that Bob was 100 percent correct. Glenn did turn out to be a great basketball player. At times he almost gave up on the game, but instead he stuck it out. And yes, they are "together" after more than fifty years, even though they are thousands of miles apart. I will always wonder if Glenn and Bob made some baby-to-baby connection in that adoption agency that lasted a lifetime.

Glenn Sr. and Linda had carefully preserved all of the adoption paperwork, including the information on Glenn's birth parents, his birthplace, and relevant health information about his blood relatives.

When Glenn turned 18, the family held a cookout and bonfire at which Glenn Sr. gave young Glenn the whole packet of information about the adoption, explained to him what it was, and told him that he should have it.

Glenn looked at the packet for a second, showed it to the 16-year-old girl who was his date that night, and shouted: "You are my parents! You are my only parents!" Tears welled up in his eyes, and he said emphatically that he had no interest in looking at those papers.

He then took the packet and threw it into the fire. As everyone was watching it burn, he repeated his feelings on the matter: "Why would I care? You are the only parents I have."

Glenn and Linda must have been deeply touched by Glenn's dramatic demonstration of love and loyalty.

I recently discussed with my dad the touchy subject of his adoption. I was curious as to whether he had ever tried to find his birth parents and other blood relatives. I also thought that, for health reasons, it would be good for me and my kids to have some genetic health information. I learned that my dad never wanted to know anything about his adoption. Absolutely nothing. He was never even curious about his birth parents. To this day he says he never thought about it while he was growing up, and he has never looked back.

In 74 years, the only time the identity of his birth parents ever crossed my dad's mind was recently when we had a medical scare. The doctors said it would be helpful to know the medical history of his birth parents. Reluctantly, Glenn went back to Waverly to try and find the information. The agency told him that the records would never be available. All the records from the 1930s and1940s were lost, gone forever. My dad felt a sense of relief, because he really did not want to know.

I asked my dad if he ever even looked at the information before he threw it into the fire. He hadn't. But someone else had gotten a good enough look at the documents to learn one interesting thing.

Bob Richards and the note he penned in 1954 to Glenn.

photo to the right: Did my dad really start his basketball career in a garage by shooting into a peach basket? Yes, he did. My dad holding the basketball with some neighborhood friends.

Glenn Borland in 1954, he was called the "clever court ace" of the Oelwein Huskies.

## Gem B: GLENN, GLENN, GLENN, AND GLENDA

This story has no shortage of Glenns. In just two chapters, I have introduced three of them. So, to put the Glenns in perspective, here's a primer.

Glenn Nicholson and his wife Ruth were the parents of the four Nicholson girls and one son. They lived on a farm just outside of Maynard, Iowa. He was my maternal grandfather and Ruth was my maternal grandmother, as their daughter Carolyn was my mother.

Glenn Borland is my father. He is the adopted son of Glenn Borland Sr. and his wife Linda. Glenn grew up in Oelwein, Iowa. Glenn Borland Sr. and his wife Linda adopted Glenn Borland, who became my father. Glenn Borland Sr. was a foreman on a railroad crew in Oelwein.

In addition to all of those Glenns, there is Glenda. Glenda is the youngest daughter of Glenn and Ruth Nicholson. She was named Glenda because Glenn and Ruth thought she was going to be a boy. And they would have named him Glenn.

M.J. Moore who was the football coach was the first coach for the new Maynards girls team in 1950-51.

Bill Mehle, who coached Maynard for three seasons put Carolyn on the High School team when she was in eighth grade.

THE FISH sisters sit down and discuss the many and varied methods of offensive play. Here, Marjorie, a starting forward, shows her sister her style on her deadly set shot. Listening attentively is Dorothy, who is a reserve forward and guard on the squad. (Photos by Olson.)

Photo courtesy of the Oelwein Daily Register

## CHAPTER 3
## OUT OF THE BARN AND INTO THE GYM

On a summer day in 1950, Carolyn Nicholson ran home to the family farmhouse bursting with excitement for, she had some news. A family from elsewhere in Iowa had bought a farm just two miles west of Maynard. Their name was Fish, and, like the Nicholsons, they had four daughters. What's more, the Fish girls, like the Nicholson girls, loved basketball. For the Nicholsons, things were looking up. Maybe.

The girls had gotten their hopes up before. In the late 1940s, when their father, Glenn, was elected to the Maynard School Board, the girls figured that with him on the board Maynard was a cinch to finally get a girls' basketball team. But their hopes were dashed when the board rejected Glenn's plea for a team.

The reason given for the rejection: Maynard didn't have enough girls who would go out for a team. But now, with the arrival of the Fish girls, Marjorie, Dorothy, Barb, and Karen, there was new hope.

For years the Nicholson girls had been playing basketball in the hayloft of their barn and in their gravel driveway. Don Fish, father of the Fish girls, built a basket and backboard and put it in the corn crib on the Fish farm. Barb Fish remembers always having to clear out the corn so that she and her sisters could play. She remembers wearing gloves, jackets, and hats as they played all winter long.

In addition to playing in their barn, the Nicholson girls would sometimes play at area parks against girls who played on teams at other schools. That was bittersweet for the Nicholson girls, because they tended to run circles around the girls from other schools. But the other girls would tease them about not having a team: "Go back to the farm and play against each other. You don't even have a team, and you're not good enough to play on one anyway." That was frustrating. All the Nicholson girls wanted was a chance to play in high school, just like those girls they would destroy on the local park courts.

In that summer of 1950, as the girls were playing on

their farms, Glenn had another go at the school board on the matter of a girls' team. This time he had an ally; Don Fish joined Glenn in some aggressive lobbying of the board and the city of Maynard.

The girls were on pins and needles. The members of the school board were concerned. Like many people in authority all over the country, they were skittish about the possibility that sports could be harmful for girls. And they continued to be concerned that a local girl had died playing basketball in the 1920s, although my grandmother, Ruth Nicholson, said it was a ruptured appendix, not basketball, that caused the girl's death. To make them more at ease with any decision they might make to restore basketball, the board members sought and got documents that included medical reports attesting that there were no exceptional risks to girls playing sports.

Despite their reservations, the board voted to resurrect the Maynard Blue Devils girls' basketball program, to start in the fall of 1950.

The girls were deliriously happy. And they were eternally grateful to their fathers.

Glenn and Don were well aware of the talent their daughters had. This awareness led them to push really hard for a Maynard team. No one could have predicted, least of all Glenn, Don, and the Nicholson and Fish girls, what a major impact they would have on the history of Iowa girls' basketball. Throughout the 1950s, Maynard teams tended to have multiple Fish and Nicholson girls. The Nicholson girls would play from 1950-1957 and the Fish girls from 1952-1959.

As the 1950-'51 season dawned, Maynard High had its girls' team, and that team had players and an enthusiastic fan base. What it didn't have was a coach. The Maynard football coach, M. J. Moore, who laid no claim to being a basketball wizard, graciously agreed to step into the void and coach the team.

As expected, the Maynard girls struggled in their first year of competition. But Maynard girls' basketball was back. While Carolyn and Glenda had two and three years before they would be in high school, Betty Nicholson was a sophomore.

My aunt Lou Ann got to play only one year for Maynard, as she graduated in 1951. She did, however, set the Nicholson-Fish train rolling down the track. In that first year, Maynard managed to finish with 10 wins and 9 losses. Not a bad start.

For the next season, 1951-'52, Maynard landed a bona fide basketball coach, Bill Mehle, who had a glittering credential: He had just coached Hansell to the state championship the year before. The girls were excited about having an experienced and successful coach who could fine-tune their skills.

That year Betty Nicholson was a junior, Carolyn was in the eighth grade and Glenda was in seventh grade. One day, during the first week of practice, the new coach asked Carolyn to come to his office.

"I know you're only in eighth grade," he told her, "but I want you to come to practice tonight and try out."

On her way to the practice, Carolyn was scared. She was not only young, she was only 5'4". She showed up at the practice, played hard, did her best, and went home after practice without talking to the coach. She cried on the way home because she felt she wasn't good enough to play with the older girls. She thought that the practice was a one-day trial, so she didn't go back the next day.

The day after she missed the practice, Coach Mehle called her back into his office and scolded her for not showing up.

Carolyn said, "When you didn't talk to me after practice, I assumed I wasn't good enough and you didn't want me back." Mehle asked her, "Do you want to play basketball, or milk cows?"

He then phoned Glenn and Ruth and said, "I want Carolyn on this team."

"She's only in the eighth grade," Ruth replied.

"I know," Mehle said, "however I said to Carolyn, 'I expect you here every day.'"

All those years of playing against her older, bigger sisters in the hayloft had paid off.

Carolyn didn't crack the starting lineup until later in the year. She ended up playing in most of the games, sometimes against girls who were five years older. In her first game, she scored 14 points. Decades later, when I asked her what she remembered about that first game, she just looked at me and smiled. For the season, against mostly juniors and seniors, my mom, as an eighth grader scored 125 points.

Under Bill Mehle that year, the Maynard Blue Devils finished with 16 wins and 4 losses. For the following season, with several starters returning, the team and its fans had great expectations.

My mom Carolyn Nicholson at left, in the 8th grade.
Photo courtesy of the Oelwein Daily Register

## CHAPTER 4
## THE IOWA GIRL AND HER GAME

James Naismith invented the game of basketball in 1891 at the Springfield, Massachusetts, YMCA. Girls in Iowa were probably not high on his list of considerations at the time. That these young girls would embrace his game so enthusiastically and create one of the most popular girls' sporting events in history was likely beyond the pale of his expectations, let alone the life-changing experiences the game would engender for generations of Iowa girls.

Just seven years after Naismith invented the game, the "Iowa Girl" was enthusiastically embracing it. Iowa girls started playing organized basketball in Dubuque in 1898. At first, they tried to play by the rules that Naismith had established. But his game and his rules were most likely invented for men, so the girls started playing by various sets of their own rules, until in 1899 the National Committee of Women's Basketball was formed to draw up rules specifically for girls. [1]

Under those new rules:
- The court was divided into three separate courts.
- Each team consisted of six players on the floor at any time, two forwards, two guards, one jumping center, and one running center.
- Jumping and contact were not allowed.
- The girls could not steal the ball or block any shots.

Under those rules, the games tended to be very "ladylike," and, even though not much defense was permitted, they tended to be low scoring. [2]

---

1 Petersen, William J. 1968. The Palimpsest, Vol. XLIX No. 4 Page 113 The State Historical Society of Iowa, April 1968

2 Chisholm, R.H. 1968. The Palimpsest, Vol. XLIX No. 4 Page 130 The State Historical Society of Iowa, April 1968

Very few fouls were called and girls were encouraged
not to make contact. The uniforms were very conservative;
according to the Palimpsest, published in April 1968, William J.
Petersen reported the girls wore "pleated black bloomers, white
or colored middies, long dark ties." They also wore full length
black stockings with black tennis slippers. Those uniforms
showed very little skin. Most of the uniforms were homemade,
as mothers of the girls would get together before the season to
make them.

Most of the gyms where the girls played in those early
days were so small that the walls were out of bounds.
In the early 1900s, girls' basketball started to get popular in
Iowa. Towns like Davenport, Ottumwa, and others got excited
about it. The following schedule and results were recorded by
the Davenport High School Blackhawk in 1908.

> Davenport 14  West Liberty 25
> Davenport 13  Lyons 19
> Davenport 17  Augustana College 3
> Davenport 27  Lyons 6
> Davenport 14  West Liberty 12

3

Obviously the Davenport girls got a lot better as the season
progressed.

The first annual Iowa girls' high school basketball tournament was held in 1920 in Des Moines. Twenty-seven invita-
tions were sent out to girls' teams throughout the state, and
twenty-four teams competed in the tournament.
According to The Palimpsest they were:

- Afton
- Albia
- Attica
- Audubon
- Churdan
- College Springs
- Correctionville

3 Petersen, William J. 1968. The Palimpsest, Vol. XLIX No.4 Page 120 The State Historical Society of Iowa, April 1968

- Dallas Center
- Fertile
- Fonda
- Garner
- Hampton
- Hiteman
- Linn Grove
- Lohrville
- Mingo
- Mount Ayr
- Nevada
- Norwalk
- Radcliffe
- Renwick
- Sheffield
- Valley Junction
- Waukee

4

The fact that few people outside of Iowa have ever heard of those towns shows how popular girls' basketball was in small towns. And little did those 24 schools know what they had just started: one of the most successful girls' sporting events in the history of the United States.

Those schools, except the ones that were close to Des Moines, faced the challenge of raising the money to travel to Des Moines for the tournament. One school that had to scrape up donations from fans and local businesses was Correctionville High, in the Sioux City area at the far western edge of the state. The town got its name because it is on the site of a surveyor's correction line. The team, however, didn't seem to need a lot of correction, because it had been undefeated for the three seasons leading up to the tournament. And Correctionville went on to win the tournament, beating Nevada 11-4 in the championship game.

The tiny town of Maynard came in for some of the glory

---

4 Petersen, William J. 1968. The Palimpsest, Vol. XLIX No.4 Page 122-123 The State Historical Society of Iowa, April 1968

in the mid-1920s, as Irene Silka led her Maynard team to the state tournament in 1924. The Maynard girls lost their first tournament game, 20-14, as Irene had an off night. However, two years later in 1926 Irene Silka would score 110 points in a single game.

In the 1920s, the popularity of girls' basketball continued to build throughout Iowa, and the girls' game was also starting to attract more national attention. But not all of that attention, in Iowa and elsewhere, was positive. In the early 1920s, even though the no-contact rule was being taken very seriously, several male and female doctors warned a nervous public that physical activity by women was dangerous and had gone too far in Iowa. Then in 1925, a national movement against girls playing sports sprang up. Its advocates held that physical sports like basketball were dangerous for girls and should be stopped. Many heated debates took place on the safety and morals of girls playing sports. An example of how the moral issue played out is the comment of one coach, as recorded by R.H. Chrisholm in The Palimpsest: "I coached girls' basketball once, and my conscience has bothered me ever since for the harm I might have done the girls." [5]

Across the country the boys' game gained in popularity while the status of the girls' programs declined.

Most other states didn't have a girls' basketball program that was as successful as the one in Iowa. But in 1925 the Iowa High School Athletic Association (IHSAA) was adamant that boys' athletics should have priority over girls' athletics. The IHSAA also said that boys' games were worthy of paid admission, while girls' games were not. The association also expressed concern that the girls were taking up valuable gym time and space that could be put to better use by the boys, a claim that would be ridiculous today.

[6] In 1926, the IHSAA, having bought into the thinking of the national movement that was claiming sports were not

5 Chisholm, R.H. 1968. The Palimpsest, Vol. XLIX No. 4 Page 125 The State Historical Society of Iowa, April 1968

6 Chisholm, R.H. 1968. The Palimpsest, Vol. XLIX No.4 Page 125 The State Historical Society of Iowa, April 1968

appropriate for girls, was determined to put an end to girls' sports in Iowa.

That stance of the IHSAA led M.M. McIntire, Claude Sankey, and the fiery John W. Agans and several others who knew and understood how important girls' athletics were to the small communities of Iowa, to fight for the girls' game. They implored the IHSAA not to discontinue girls' basketball. At a meeting of the IHSAA board, John W. Agans, of Mystic, Iowa, stood up and shouted at the board members a prophecy that would resound for decades all over Iowa. The Palimpsest reported that he said: "Gentlemen, if you attempt to do away with girls' basketball in Iowa, you'll be standing in the center of the track when the train runs over you!" [7]

But the IHSAA voted to drop all girls' sports from the association and refused to support any girls' events.

Almost immediately, Agans' prophecy started to come true. The twenty-five men – mostly school principals, school superintendents, and coaches banded together in 1926 to form the Iowa Girls High School Athletic Union (IGHSAU). This new entity created its own rules and acted independently.

Most states were in step with the anti-girls'-sports sentiment, and they did not let girls play school sports. So the IGHSAU was truly on its own. As the IGHSAU grew, there was a tremendous amount of friction between the two Iowa associations. It was literally boys' programs vs. girls' programs.

The IGHSAU's crown jewel was the annual Girls' State Basketball Tournament. The IGHSAU hosted its first sponsored State Tournament in 1926 at Hampton, Iowa.

From 1926-1930, the annual tournament would rotate from town to town. But most towns had limited facilities for hosting such a big event. This was the era of dirt and gravel roads, which made it challenging for teams and fans to get to the tournament. And it was obvious that they needed a bigger venue. The games were held in small gyms that were packed to the rafters with enthusiastic fans. The demand was there, the

7 Chisholm, R.H. 1968. The Palimpsest, Vol. XLIX No. 4 Page 125-126 The State Historical Society of Iowa, April 1968

girls just needed more space.

In the 1931 season, the IGHSAU moved the State Tournament to the Drake Field House in Des Moines. It had a capacity of 7,000, and every one of those seats was needed because of the continually increasing popularity of the girls' game. The new tournament format would involve 16 teams, and Iowa was calling the teams the sweet sixteen many years before the NCAA picked up on that expression.

During the 1930s and 40s the girls' game had gotten so popular in rural Iowa that an estimated 70 percent of the teams came from small communities. Most girls who had any interest in playing a sport went out for basketball, as that was the only girls' sport that was offered. Girls who didn't have the ability to make the team could be team managers or cheerleaders.

By this time, John Agans' comments were beginning to look like an understatement. Boys' basketball in Iowa would have a hard time reaching the heights of popularity and excitement of Iowa girls' basketball.

The next significant year was 1934. That year, in the depth of the Depression, the IGHSAU decided to change the rules. The rule changes they made transformed Iowa 6 on 6 basketball and would take Iowa girls' basketball to almost unbelievable heights of popularity. The new rules would last from 1934-1941.

They were unique — and very effective. Following is a summary of the new rules:

- Each team played six players at a time, three offense/forwards and three defense/guards. (The 6 on 6 wasn't new, but the roles of the players had been shifted.)
- Each player could only play on half of the court. The offense/forwards only played offense on one half of the court and the defense/guards only played defense on the other half of the court when the other team was on offense.
- An offensive player could only dribble two times before she had to pass or shoot, and she only had three seconds to make that decision. This rule made for fast-paced

games.

- After one team would make a basket, a referee would quickly take the ball and pass it to the other ref at half court, who would hand it to one of the offensive players on the other team to re-start play.
- If the offensive team missed and the other team got the rebound, those offensive players would press or try to keep the other team's defensive players from getting the ball to half court for the transition pass to the offense. Like the offensive players, a defensive player could only dribble two times before having to pass the ball.

But in 1941, with the new rules in place the game changed again. The guards were now encouraged and coached to play physical, they were taught how to aggressively steal the ball, tie up the ball, and block shots. [8]

In other words, they could play real defense. The game suddenly became much more physical and more competitive. Many argued that scoring would go way down. But the scoring actually went up as players developed more quickness and finesse. The forwards could still only dribble two times, but the defenders/guards could steal the ball. Same was true when the offensive team missed, those offensive players now became defenders, and they were allowed to steal the ball.

In the 1950 rule book The Palimpsest cited "about 30 differences in the boys' and girls' game." [9] It was at this time that the boys' Union was pushing the IGHSAU to adapt to the boys' game and merge the boys' and girls' rules. But the IGHSAU would have none of that. They thought they had a better game. Their new rules would last for over fifty years, and those were the rules that were in effect when the Nicholson girls played.

Along with new rules, came new uniforms. Out went the stodgy bloomers, in came the more attractive and fashionable

8 Chisholm, R.H. 1968. The Palimpsest, Vol. XLIX No.4 Page 130 The State Historical Society of Iowa, April 1968

9 Chisholm, R.H. 1968. The Palimpsest, Vol. XLIX No.4 Page 131 The State Historical Society of Iowa, April 1968

shorts or skirts.

The increased action of the girls' game led to yet another major surge in the game's popularity. The new version of the 6 on 6 game was a totally different game from the old girls' game, and it was far more exciting and far more popular than the boys' 5 on 5 game. It was not uncommon to see hundreds or even thousands of spectators at girls' regular season games. In some cases, the boys would follow the girls' games, and only 50-100 people out of a girls'-game crowd of more than 1,000 would stay for the boys' game. The girls' games were faster, higher scoring, and sometimes more physical.

During the early years, the Des Moines Tribune, led by Jack North, started covering girls' games, and that fed the growing craze. Chuck Offenburger of the Des Moines Register also became a huge supporter of girls' 6 on 6 basketball. In most cases, entire towns would support their team. Almost every girl in Iowa wanted a chance to play. The hearts of the entire state were behind "The Iowa Girl," considered by many to be the luckiest girl in the country.

The popularity of girls' basketball in Iowa was unmatched anywhere else. It was estimated that more than 700 high schools in Iowa had 6 on 6 teams and in the 1950s more than 70% of all Iowa girls played 6 on 6 basketball. Another state that did have a strong girls' basketball program was Texas. As in Iowa, Texas girls played 6 on 6. In 1948, Iowa played host to a Texas team. For the game between Kamrar of Iowa and Mesquite of Texas, 7,000 fans filled Drake Field House and watched the Iowa team win 36-33.

[10]     More than 40,000 fans attended the 1949 girls' State Tournament, but many who wanted tickets couldn't get them. It was apparent that even the Drake Field House wasn't big enough. The new tournament site, as of 1955, would be Veterans Memorial Auditorium in Des Moines, with a capacity of 15,000 and the nickname of The Big Barn.

According to Jim Duncan, who wrote for The Palimp-

10 Chisholm, R.H. 1968. The Palimpsest, Vol. XLIX No.4 Page 143 The State Historical Society of Iowa, April 1968

sest, WOI-TV of Ames, Iowa televised the first girls' high school basketball game in 1951 and an estimated 260,000 viewers tuned in. He also reported that in 1955 thirty newspapers and twenty-five radio stations covered the State Tournament, with the play by play announcing done by Jim Zabal of 1040 WHO Radio. [11]So, as the national debate on whether girls should compete in sports roared on, Iowa girls' basketball was cruising.

The 1954-'55 season saw the arrival on the scene of a legendary figure who would steer the fortunes of Iowa girls' basketball for almost half a century. E. Wayne Cooley, who quit a job as administrative assistant to the president of Grinnell College, in Grinnell, Iowa, to become head of the IGHSAU, was more than an administrator. He was part ringmaster, part innovator, and all promoter.

Cooley was passionate in his desire to take Iowa girls' basketball, which already was immensely popular, to dizzying heights. One thing he did was to transform the girls' State Tournament into a spectacle with a carnival-like atmosphere. Cooley felt that the games were only one important element. He certainly could not 100 percent guarantee that every game would be a great one or would offer compelling matchups, but he could guarantee great entertainment. The pageantry Cooley added to the State Tournament included bands, dancers, fireworks, and boys dressed in tuxes to sweep and mop the floor at halftime. Thousands of people came to the State Tournament just to be part of Cooley's show. The tournament had become so successful that eventually CBS, USA Today, the New York Times, NBC, and Sports Illustrated all covered the event. They were all interested in reporting the phenomenon that was Iowa girls' basketball. During the height of the popularity the girls' tournament would earn higher TV ratings statewide than network shows. It was so popular that in 1966 an estimated 5 million viewers from nine surrounding states watched telecasts of the girls' tournament. In 1973 Sports Illustrated ran a series covering the Iowa 6 on 6 game. They wanted to understand how the IGHSAU was

11 Duncan, Jim. 1968. The Palimpsest, Vol. XLIX No.4 Page 147 The State Historical Society of Iowa, April 1968

making the girls' game so popular. Iowa was the model of equality and proof to the nation that girls were equal to boys.
The tournament and the 6 on 6 style of play was so exciting that one announcer who covered the men's NCAA tournament games proclaimed that the Iowa girls' tournament was much more exciting and electric than the NCAA tournament.

One of Cooley's many achievements was the coining of the expression "the Iowa girl," and linking it to Iowa girls' basketball. And everything he did was in the interest of celebrating the Iowa girl. He was adamant that the Iowa girl was not secondary to the boys and their game.

At one point, a national network wanted to buy the rights to the Iowa girls' State Tournament. Cooley and the IGHSAU turned them down, as they did not want to give up any control of their crown jewel. Cooley strongly believed that the Iowa girl should stand alone.

In 1973 Sports Illustrated reported, "All those dire warnings of the medical, moral, and financial disasters that would follow if girls were granted athletic parity are considered hogwash in Iowa ... In fact there may be no place in the United States where sport is so healthy and enjoys such good reputation."
[12]

*The Head Man*

**E. WAYNE COOLEY**
Executive Secretary

Photo courtesy of IGHSAU

---

12 Williamson, N. Gilbert, B  "Women in Sport, Are You Being Two-Faced?" Sports Illustrated June , 4, 1973

HERE'S THE 1924 Maynard girls basketball team that went to the state tourna
Lehmkuhl Sisk, Waterloo. Seated: Christine Froning aack, Maynard; Irene Silka Be
Lemkuhl Sisk, Waterloo. Seated: Christine Froning and Verna Silka Speak, Geor

1924 Maynard team. Photo courtesy of IGHSAU

In the 1950s, not only new rules but new
style uniforms.
Photo courtesy of IGHSAU

This is how they sta
1920s.
Photo courtesy of IC

## Gem C: SOME OF THE HOGWASH

Iowa Public Television produced a documentary, "More than a Game 6-on-6 Basketball in Iowa." In the documentary they reported the following:

In 1945, the National Federation of State High School Athletic Associations, who managed boys' athletics in thirty-nine states, actually made the following statement in its handbook:

> "It is doubtful whether the skills or mental characteristics, which result from engaging in strenuous widely publicized contests is conducive to the development of those characteristics which are associated with cultured womanhood."

13

---

13 More Than a Game 6 on 6 Basketball in Iowa : Iowa Public Television Documentary Video.
photo to the left: Carolyn Nicholson driving to the basket in 8th grade.
Photo courtesy of the Oelwein Daily Register

Photo courtesy of the Oelwein Daily Register

The bright spot in the Maynard defeat was freshman Carolyn Nicholson's brilliant offensive show. The forward popped in 21 points, the majority of which came on set shots. To date, this was her best performance.

THE NICHOLSON sisters (left to right), Carolyn, Betty and Glenda group together as they get a chance to talk over their team's chances in the coming district tourney. Carolyn and Betty are regulars and Glenda, who is in eighth grade, is a reserve on the Blue Devilettes.

Photo courtesy of the Oelwein Daily Register

# CHAPTER 5
## KNOCKING ON THE DOOR

The 1952-'53 season, Bill Mehle's second as the Maynard coach, was a special year for the Nicholson girls and their
parents, as three Nicholson girls got to play on the same team.
Betty Nicholson was now a senior, Carolyn was a freshman,
Glenda was an 8th grader, and, as he did with Carolyn, the
coach added Glenda to the high school team while she was in
the 8th grade.

The team also had a star forward in junior Marjorie
Fish. Her sister Dorothy was a freshman. Also on that team was
freshman Marlene Becker, nicknamed Snooky. Betty took on the
leadership role that Lou Ann had left her, and Betty and Marjorie showed their talented younger sisters the way.

Late in the season, Roger Olson of the Oelwein Daily
Register wrote a column titled "Maynard's Bill Mehle 'Likes
Varsity Sisters.'" It read in part:

"If blood relations mean anything to the success of a
basketball team there is one registerland coach who will
give a hearty "I like sisters" whenever he can.

That coach is Maynard's very successful Bill Mehle
who can boast five girls on his club that come from two
families. The girls, the Nicholson and Fish sisters, make
up the regular forward court and a part of the reserve
strength on the Maynard Blue Devilettes.

In the Nicholson trio of sisters Betty, a 17-year-old
senior, leads the team in scoring from her post forward
position, Carolyn a 15-year-old freshman, handles one
forward, scoring well and doing a tremendous job of
feeding her teammates. Glenda, a 13-year-old 8th grade
student, is a reserve and sees considerable action, especially during this later stage of the season.

The two other sisters, Marjorie and Dorothy Fish, complete the quintet on the Mehle varsity team. Marjorie, a

16-year-old junior, teams with the two Nicholsons at forward in the offensive plan. Using a deadly set shot and speedy drive-ins to advantage she has greatly aided the Maynard surge to statewide notice in girls' cage circles. Her sister, a 14-year-old freshman, is a fine offensive player and has been used occasionally by Mehle as a guard also."

Toward the end of the regular season, the three Nicholson girls were pictured in the local paper. The caption read: "The Nicholson sisters Carolyn, Betty and Glenda group together as they get a chance to talk over their team's chances in the coming district tournament. Carolyn and Betty are regulars, and Glenda, who is in 8th grade, is a reserve on the Blue Devilettes."

Led by the Nicholson and Fish girls, Maynard had a great regular season. They started the season 18-0, then faced the mighty Garnavillo team, led by stars Sandy Fiete and Jean Overbeck. Garnavillo is a town in the next county east of Maynard's Fayette County. It's just a few miles from the Mississippi River, it has traditionally had a few more people than Maynard, and its girls' basketball team was a powerhouse.

Against Garnavillo, Carolyn had her best game of the season, scoring 21 points. That wasn't enough. Maynard lost 59-47.

Sandy Fiete led Garnavillo with 22 points. For Maynard, in addition to Carolyn's 21 points, Betty and Marjorie Fish each got 13. Nobody else scored for Maynard.

Maynard would see Garnavillo again - in the district tournament.

Of Carolyn's performance, Rodger Olson of the Daily Register wrote:

"The bright spot in the Maynard defeat was Freshman Carolyn Nicholson's brilliant offensive show. The forward popped in 21 points, the majority of which came on set shots. To date this was her best performance."

Later in Carolyn's freshman season, Rodger Olson again reported on Carolyn's potential:

"Ably assisting in the play of the forward court is Carolyn Nicholson, the Maynard freshman flash. Although only a frosh athlete, she is in her second year as a regular and has shown an adept ability to play under pressure. Boasting a large display of good shots, she is destined to become one of the bright spots on the cage scene."

Maynard, which ended its regular season with a 24-1 record, sailed through its sectional games and was two wins away from the State Tournament. In the district semifinal, they would play Lamont.

As expected Maynard breezed past Lamont 66-37. Majorie Fish led the way with 32 points, Carolyn scored 18, Betty 16, again the only three to score. The winner of the next game, the district final, would get a berth in the State Tournament. The opponent would be Garnavillo.

Maynard now had the opportunity to exact revenge against the only team to beat them all season. It would be a major challenge to topple mighty Garnavillo, however. Coaches around the area predicted an easy Garnavillo victory.

Could the young Maynard team pull the upset? No. It wasn't even close. The Maynard season ended as Garnavillo rolled over the Blue Devilettes 61-39. There is a picture of the girls walking off the floor, the scoreboard in the background reading 61-39. Garnavillo had found Maynard's weakness: they were young, inexperienced and unaccustomed to physical play. The Oelwein Daily Register reported Garnavillo Coach Louis Daily as saying "There were so many jump balls in the first period that I decided to have my girls play a bit rougher and it seemed to pay off."

It would be the last time the three Nicholson sisters would play together. They would finish with a record of 27-2.

Garnavillo went on to win the 1953 state championship. It was a bit of a consolation to the Maynard girls that they had lost to the best team in the state. But still it was a loss, and a lopsided one at that.

Betty, who had a great senior year, was selected third team all-state. Throughout the season it was obvious that the two younger Nicholson girls were very special, even as eighth

and ninth graders. Carolyn, as a freshman starter, scored 389
points on the season and was one of the team's best players.
Glenda got valuable experience as an eighth grader. Freshman
Marlene Becker had a productive year, scoring 99 points. Maynard had fielded a very good team that season, but they were
young.

Betty was Maynard's only starter not returning for the
next season. It would be up to Carolyn and Glenda to carry the
Nicholson torch. They were very optimistic going into the next
year. In that 1953-'54 season, Maynard still was a young team.
Carolyn was a sophomore and Glenda a freshman. The high
scoring Marjorie Fish was back for her senior season, and Marlene "Snooky" Becker and Dorothy Fish were now sophomores.
The defense was led by a talented freshman, 5'8" Dorothy Fettkether. The starting six included three sophomores, two freshmen, and one senior.

The young Maynard team had another tremendous year
ending up with a record of 23-4. While the four losses were an
increase from the prior season, the Blue Devilettes played a
tougher schedule in '53-'54. This, combined with their youth,
increased the degree of difficulty, a challenge to which the girls
rose admirably. They would average 64 points per game and
give up only 49. Carolyn led the team in scoring with 724 points,
followed by Marjorie Fish with 546. Sophomore Snooky Becker
had a nice season at the forward position scoring 297 points.
Carolyn's 724 points in a season was a Maynard record. She
accomplished this as a sophomore.

In the postseason tournament, Maynard again rolled
through the sectionals, winning three games by an average of 23
points. In the district final, they would, for the second year in a
row, face mighty Garnavillo. Maynard again was only one win
away from a berth in the State Tournament.

Heartbreak would set in again as Garnavillo beat Maynard 68-48. Garnavillo would go back to back and win the state
tournament again in 1954. Years later, Carolyn recalled that the
young Maynard team was no match for the powerful Garnavillo
team, which she called "extraordinary."

Two years in a row, the best team in the state shattered

Maynard's dream to play in the State Tournament.

Several major events unfolded after that season-ending loss to Garnavillo. Carolyn, after scoring 724 points as a sophomore, was voted 4th team all-state. On March 12, 1954 she received a letter from Rodger Olson of the Oelwein Daily Register congratulating her on the award. In addition to the congratulations, the letter conveyed the sentiment that Carolyn would face a great deal of pressure to advance girls' basketball and also implied that she may begin to experience jealousy from surrounding players as one of only two sophomores on the 32-girl list. A comment in the letter simply said, "The honor is obvious and the challenge is for you to work harder, both on and off the court, to advance girls' basketball in Maynard and those cities and towns in which you play." Two years later Carolyn Nicholson would be credited with revolutionizing the out-forward position in Iowa girls' basketball.

Another major event was the revelation that the successful and popular Bill Mehle would not return to coach Maynard. The team did not know why. Carolyn thought the coach quit because he didn't think they were good enough and was disappointed in them after the losses to Garnavillo. Only years later would she and the others learn that Mehle had been let go in a dispute with the school administration, and that it had nothing to do with the talent of the team and the losses to Garnavillo.

When the girls found out that Coach Mehle wasn't coming back they were absolutely crushed. They loved playing for him. Now what? The only key player lost to the Maynard team was Marjorie Fish. The young Maynard team had gained valuable playing experience, and the nucleus was coming back: juniors Carolyn Nicholson, Marlene "Snooky" Becker, and Dorothy Fish and sophomores Glenda Nicholson and Dorothy Fettkether.

They were anxious for the season to start. But they had no idea who would coach the team or how he would mesh with the chemistry they had developed in prior years. They were still shocked by Mehle's departure, and they were looking for direction.

In the fall of 1954 Mel Kupferschmid arrived on the

Maynard scene. He was a seasoned coach who turned out to be
the perfect fit, exactly what the talented Maynard team needed.
He came from Mount Union, a nearby town, where he had
already been a successful coach. He actually had been hired to
be the principal at Maynard.

The school's administration decided that he also would
coach girls' basketball. Most of the girls knew of him and had
heard good things about him.

When Coach Kupferschmid arrived in Maynard, a lot of
pressure was put on him to continue the success of the program.
When asked about the Maynard team and about his new job, he
was quoted as saying, "I know I have the Nicholson sisters for
the next two years. Maynard will be good."

Coach Kupferschmid recently told me that after the first
practice with his new team, he knew he had walked into "something special." During that first practice he also couldn't believe
how small the Maynard gymnasium was. There was no room to
take the ball out of bounds under the basket. The fans all had to
be packed into a balcony that overlooked the tiny old gym.

Coach Kupferschmid did a fantastic job. The girls loved
him. He was a basketball guy, a great coach and a "very intel-
ligent man," according to Carolyn. She remembered her new
coach always challenging her to one-on-one games. She also
recalled her new coach during practice making Glenda shoot
baskets by herself on the side for hours and hours.

The 1954-'55 season was a huge success. The Maynard
team went 22-3, averaged 72 points per game and gave up 52
points per game. The three losses resulted from yet another step
up in scheduling difficulty. Further, "Coach Koop," as some of
the girls called him, spent a lot of time building team chemistry
and learning his players' strengths and weaknesses. Carolyn had
another great year as Maynard's leading scorer, ringing up 837
points for the season. Glenda Nicholson was the second leading
scorer with 563 points.

Carolyn would be voted third team all-state. Dorothy
Fish and Glenda Nicholson were voted honorable mention.
A paragraph in the Maynard statistics book stated: "Carolyn
Nicholson broke Irene Silka's Maynard all-time scoring mark

of 1,707 points. Carolyn now had 2,075 points. Carolyn broke her own single season scoring record of 724 points with 837 this season." Carolyn Nicholson was a rising star in the state of Iowa.

At tournament time, expectations were at an all-time high. For the third year in a row, Maynard would cruise through the early playoff rounds beating teams by 20 plus points. In the district semifinals, Maynard would play St. Francis De Sales, of Ossian, Iowa, with the winner set to play Monona for the right to go to the State Tournament.

Against De Sales, the Maynard girls rolled on, winning 86-64. The headline over Ernie Eschbach's story in the Oelwein Daily Register read: "C. Nicholson top scorer hits 52 points." Eschbach story said:

"Spearheading the attack for Maynard was Carolyn Nicholson, a smooth, tricky, hard driving forward who poured in 20 of the first 30 points and accounted for 52 points for the game.

The victory wasn't a one-girl show, though. Post-forward Glenda Nicholson, showing a future promise with a good hook shot took up where her sister left off, tossing 29 points through the hoop."

The sisters scored an incredible 81 of the team's 86 points, leading the Blue Devilettes to victory. With the blowout win against a very good De Sales team, Maynard knew they would likely soon face Monona. They would find themselves in the district final for the third year in a row, just one more win away from fulfilling their childhood dreams of playing in the State Tournament. Standing in their way, as predicted, was a solid Monona team that Maynard had beaten twice during the regular season, 70- 67 and 55-54, both very close, competitive games.

Monona was a very good team, and it had become even stronger when superstar Jean Overbeck transferred from mighty Garnavillo to Monona. That transfer had shifted the balance of power in the area, a fact that was borne out when, earlier in the tournament, Monona played Garnavillo. Garnavillo still

had the brilliant Sandy Fiete. But Jean Overbeck and her new
Monona teammates beat the powerful, two-time defending state
champions, knocking them out of the tournament.

Although the Maynard girls knew Monona was no
pushover, the elimination of their nemesis Garnavillo, plus the
fact that they had beaten Monona twice that season made them
confident. Maynard was favored to beat Monona and go to the
State Tournament for the first time in over thirty-five years, and
only five years since the Maynard girls' basketball program was
resurrected.

The entire town of Maynard, including all of the stores,
shut down, and everybody turned out for the game. Those fans
watched the Maynard girls get off to an uncharacteristically
slow start. Maynard and its fans had a bad feeling about what
was going to happen, and that bad feeling proved prophetic, as
the Maynard girls were never able to overcome the slow start.

My mom never talked much about this game. Nor does
Glenda, as it is obviously too painful to think about. My mom
teared up when I asked her what happened in that game. "The
entire team played like we were dead," she said. "No player even
broke a sweat." After playing their worst game in three years,
the Maynard girls shuffled off the court in a trance of disbelief.
They simply wondered how they could play so badly, as Monona
beat favored Maynard 68-51.

For the first time, Glenn Nicholson was angry with his
daughters over the way they played. He was a proud man. He
wore a suit and tie to every game he attended. He typically
didn't get involved, but this time he felt his daughters had let
the entire town of Maynard down. "How could you beat that
team twice during the season and play so bad in the most
important game of your life?" he asked.

Carolyn was already upset as she knew Maynard had
the better team and should have been going to the state tournament. Glenda recently recalled the conversation they had as
they were sitting in their living room getting scolded by their
father. Glenda believes her dad was hurt and embarrassed by
how badly his daughters had played. And she remembers how
Carolyn, for the first time ever, confronted her strict, angry

father, saying to him, "We play for our coach and not for you."

Glenda was shocked at her response and realized it had taken a lot of courage for her sister to stand up to their father. That shows how well liked and well respected Coach Kupferschmid was by his team.

After their loss to Monona, the Maynard girls began a soul-searching process that would last a lifetime: How could they have let that game slip away?

Meanwhile, Coach Kupferschmid would take several of the girls to Des Moines to watch the other teams fulfill their dreams and play in the State Tournament.

Monona lost early in the tournament, and Goldfield, a small town in north central Iowa, would end up winning the 1955 State Tournament. Carolyn and Glenda could only sit and watch the happy winners, knowing they could have been the ones doing the celebrating.

The ugly loss to Monona would haunt the girls and the entire town of Maynard for the next nine months. The bad taste did not let up. Maynard just couldn't seem to win that final game. Were they going to get another chance?

For the 1955-'56 season, Carolyn, Snooky, and Dorothy would be seniors. Carolyn was a preseason first team all-state player. Glenda, a rising star, would be a junior.

Carolyn Nicholson had one last chance to fulfill her dream that started as an 8-year-old girl shooting baskets in the hayloft on the family farm. The carvings on her bedroom wall were still there: "Maynard State Champs 1956."

Coach Kupferschmid with the star sisters Carolyn on the left and Glenda.
Photo courtesy of the Oelwein Daily Register

Glenn Borland in high school, his patented left
handed hook shot.
Photo courtesy of the Oelwein Daily Register

Dad was very popular in high school. Jim Nelson, an
art student, drew this portrait of Glenn Borland during
his junior season.

My dad's hook was unstoppable. The gym was always a full house.
Photo courtesy of the Oelwein Daily Register

# CHAPTER 6
# THE DEADLY HOOK

It was on the makeshift basketball court in the family garage in Oelwein, that my father, Glenn Borland, developed his famous and deadly left-handed hook shot.

When asked why he started shooting hook shots (the hook is a fairly uncommon shot), he explained that inside that nine car garage, a few feet in front of and above the basket, was a support beam that ran across the width of the structure. That beam guarded the basket in a way that prevented players from taking a lot of traditional shots. The beam interfered with such shots as a set shot from 20 feet.

"The best way to get the ball over that beam," Glenn said, "was to shoot a hook shot."

Glenn credits that shot as a major reason for his basketball success because he used it to score against much bigger players. Maybe those hours he spent in the garage perfecting his hook shot was the reason that Glenn, who never grew taller than six foot one and a half, became a forward instead of a guard. Glenn was known in high school and college for his unstoppable hook shot, and even today people in Oelwein and in Madison, Wisconsin, where Dad and I live, talk about that left handed hook.

He had started playing in that garage at age 10, and must have taken thousands of hook shots as he practiced there. Once Glenn reached middle school he would refine his basketball skills on the school playground two blocks from his house. Glenn played almost every day all day long, usually by himself. In the winter, he would shovel all the snow off of the outdoor basketball courts just to play. He didn't have or need the latter-day distractions of youth like TV, video games, and the Internet. All he needed was a basketball and a basket.

One Sunday afternoon Glenn and a couple of his friends snuck into the local elementary school, crawling through an opening used for dumping coal into the building, climbing down a coal pile into the furnace room, then getting into the rest of the building by going through the unlocked furnace room door.

They were there for one thing only — to play basketball. For several Sundays they did this. Each time they would play all day, and it seemed nobody was noticing. But one day when they tried to sneak in the opening was covered with a panel, and it was secured with a padlock. Glenn and his friends weren't going to let a garden variety hardware store lock interfere with their determination to play basketball. So they broke the lock. And they spent another Sunday playing basketball in the gym.

The school announced that there had been "a major break-in" over the weekend. The school said it was yet to be determined what was stolen. Nothing had been stolen, but Glenn came forward and told the principal that he and his friends had snuck into the school to play basketball. And all of the other perps of the "major break-in" eventually came forward and fessed up, too. The boys went unpunished, and they were praised for their honesty.

Glenn attended Oelwein High School from 1951-1954. As a freshman, he played freshman football and basketball and ran track. Glenn also loved baseball, but Oelwein High did not have a baseball team. In the 1951-1952 season, as a sophomore, he made the varsity basketball team and took a starting spot away from a senior, who years later became Glenn's brother-in-law.

Oelwein's best basketball team was when Glenn was a junior. That team, led by Glenn and 6'7" senior center Ray Nisson, was 27-1. In 1953 Oelwein was one of sixteen teams that made it to the Iowa State Tournament. Back then schools weren't divided into classes based on the size of the schools. There were no classes or divisions in Iowa, so Oelwein was up against some of the biggest schools in the state.

The only regular-season loss the team had was a 1 point loss to Waverly. Two weeks later they would beat that same Waverly team by 30 points.

In the second game of the State Tournament, Glenn hurt his ankle and could play only half of the game. The team lost by 1 point in double overtime to Bishop Heelan High of Sioux City. To this day Glenn thinks that if he hadn't gotten hurt, the team would have won the 1953 Iowa State Tournament.

That year, Glenn was named first team all-conference

in basketball. He also was all-conference in football as a wide receiver and occasional kicker. He claims that he drop - kicked field goals and extra points instead of using a holder. He also ran the half mile for the track team and participated in the Drake Relays.

During the summer before his senior year Glenn was a typical small-town teenager. As his friends recently reminisced about the good old days, they recalled the drag races they had with the goal of reaching 60 mph on the back roads around Oelwein, and Glenn's friends insist that sometimes the cops would chase them.

The 1953-'54 school year was Glenn's senior year, and he was now getting statewide recognition for his basketball talent.

The season opened with a scrimmage against Sacred Heart, a Catholic school in Oelwein. This game had stirred up a lot of local interest, because Sacred Heart had a star player named Dale Kisner who averaged 30 points a game. Glenn would be guarding Kisner, and Glenn's teammates challenged him by betting him that Kisner would score more than 10 points off of him. Oelwein beat Sacred Heart by 25 points. Not only did Kisner not score 10 points, Glenn shut him out. He scored 0.

As the season went on, Glenn was an all-state selection and was dominating the league.

The team was so popular that Oelwein home games were a very tough ticket. And if you didn't get to the gym by 5 o'clock, three hours before tip-off, you couldn't get in to see the game. Many of the people who attended were there primarily to see the local star, Glenn Borland. Glenn's mom and dad would leave their house at 4:45 on game days to secure their seats.

Meanwhile Glenn and his teammates would meet at his house, make grilled cheese sandwiches, and listen to something that in the mid-1950s was in its infancy, rock 'n' roll.
At 7 o'clock, they'd leave for the game,

Throughout his senior season, Glenn was heavily recruited by a number of colleges. Although Oelwein's record was barely above .500, they made it to the Sectional Tournament final, only to suffer another tough loss in their first game, this time to Starmont High of Strawberry Point. The local star and legend had just played his last basketball game for Oelwein. It was now time to decide where to go to college.

Glenn's parents had no extra money. The only way he would be able to attend college and play basketball was on a basketball scholarship. His parents, now in their 60s, along with his coach Jack Darland, were trying to help him make the right decision.

Bucky O'Connor, the University of Iowa basketball coach, was very interested in giving Glenn a scholarship, and Iowa was where Glenn wanted to go. But the Iowa Hawkeyes, who had just won the 1954 Big Ten championship and would get all of their players back for the next season, had no scholarships available to give to anybody, including Glenn. So the Iowa offer was for Glenn to enroll at the university, not play basketball for a year and then get the full scholarship offer starting with his sophomore year. For several reasons, including having no money to pay for the first year, Glenn decided to reject the Iowa offer.

After looking at several other offers, Glenn decided to enroll at Cornell College, a private liberal arts college in Mount Vernon, Iowa. In sports, Cornell was a division three school. Cornell offered him a full scholarship beginning in his freshman year and was close to home, while Iowa did not offer any scholarship money in the first year. The proximity to Oelwein plus the scholarship won the day for Glenn. But in July, with Glenn just thirty days from starting classes at Cornell College, a combination of luck and fate would change his life forever.

John Duncan, who was from Oelwein, lived in Madison, Wisconsin, John was a good friend of Jack Darland, (Glenn's high school basketball coach,) and he was a long-time fan of Glenn. Duncan was back in Oelwein for a weekend and ran into Jack Darland. John asked Jack where Glenn was going to play basketball. Darland replied, "He is going to division three Cornell as Iowa's full scholarship offer doesn't start until next year, so Glenn decided not to take it."

A surprised and disappointed John Duncan returned to Madison that Sunday. As fate would have it, Duncan ran into the University of Wisconsin basketball coach, Bud Foster, at the

Odana golf course. He told Foster about a kid from his home town that University of Iowa's Bucky O'Connor really wanted but didn't have a scholarship to offer. Duncan told Foster that Glenn was good enough to play Big Ten basketball and that he should pursue him.

Two days later fate continued to play its hand. There was a coaches' clinic in Ames, Iowa, and both O'Connor and Foster attended it. Foster followed up on the conversation he had with Duncan just two days before about a kid from Oelwein that O'Connor had been interested in. O'Connor proceeded to tell Bud Foster, "I think Glenn Borland is good enough to play Big Ten basketball. We don't have any scholarships available this year, but we offered Glenn one for next year. He turned down our scholarship offer. Apparently he didn't want to sit out a year."

Foster took O'Connor's and Duncan's appraisals of Glenn seriously, and sent this letter to Glenn on July 19, 1954:

Dear Glen:

Mr. John Duncan of Madison, Wisconsin, who formerly came from Oelwein, Iowa, told Art Rizzi, who is our freshman basketball coach that you were interested in going to school next year.

I would like to suggest to you that the University of Wisconsin is a very fine institution, that is rated very high academically and has a fine athletic program to go along with this school.

From what I have heard of you, your grades are ample to be admitted here and I believe are high enough to receive some scholarship help if you are interested in us.

I believe that if you have any feeling toward the University of Wisconsin that it would be a good idea to pay us a visit some weekend when we can show you the school and go over any problems that you may have.

During summer months I am away from the city on a part-time traveling job but am always in the office on Saturday and at my home on Sunday.

If you are considering us and wish to pay us a visit, I would appreciate a line from you telling me when you could come here. We would be very happy to make hotel arrangements for you and also take care of your meals while you are in the city. This is according to Conference regulations and I would be very happy to meet with you and become better acquainted.

Please let me hear from you and if I can send any information in the way of a University bulletin covering some particular course please request it in the near future.

Hoping to hear from you soon, I am
Sincerely yours,
H.E. Foster
Coach of Basketball

The next letter Bud Foster wrote, dated July 26, 1954, was to Glenn's coach Jack Darland, basically saying Glenn had not responded to his original letter. It said:

Dear Mr. Darland:

Thank you very much for your letter of July 19 concerning Glen (sic - and following) Borland of Oelwein, Iowa. I received information last weekend regarding this young man from Mr. Rizzi and Mr. Wegner and wrote the boy a letter to which he has not yet replied.

I suggested to him that if he were interested in the University of Wisconsin he should come in and look us over and become acquainted with us. It would be important that he come here on a weekend as I am away from the city this summer on a traveling job during the week.

If Glen is a good student and in the top half of his graduated class, I am sure that he could be admitted here and
it would be possible to help him with his out-of-state and
in-state fees. We also have plenty of employment so that
boys can earn their room and board if they find it neces-
sary to do so.

If he is interested in the University at Madison, we are
more than willing to take an interest in him and help
him.

I certainly hope that you will pass on this information to
Glen and will hope to have an opportunity to meet him
in the near future.

Thank you again for your interest in us as well as in Glen
and I hope it will work out so that we will find him on
our campus in September.

My kindest regards to you.

Sincerely,
H.E. Foster
Coach of Basketball

It was just three weeks before Glenn was to enroll at
Cornell. Bud Foster called the Borland home in Oelwein and
finally talked to Glenn. He asked him if he would be interested
in visiting Wisconsin and maybe playing for the Badgers.

There was one problem: Glenn's parents' car would not
make the trip to Madison. They borrowed a car from Bob Richards' dad, who owned an automobile dealership, and the Borland family together made the journey to Madison.

Glenn and his parents met with Bud Foster, and Foster
told them he wanted to offer Glenn a scholarship. However,
before the offer would be official Glenn needed to pass an

entrance exam as he was short on math credits.

Glenn took the test and soon got a telegram from the University of Wisconsin congratulating him on passing the test and officially offering him a scholarship that included tuition, room, board, and a part time job as a waiter in a restaurant. But there was a catch. The scholarship they offered to Glenn was a one-year scholarship. If Glenn did not make the team after the first year, the scholarship would go away.

Glenn and his parents went back to Oelwein to think about it over the weekend. The pressure was on, because Glenn was now only two weeks away from the date by which he would have to enroll at Cornell.

Jack Darland, Glenn's high school coach told him that while he preferred Iowa, he understood that the scholarship was very important. Wisconsin was still in the Big Ten and was only a 3-hour drive away. Darland told Glenn that he "would be foolish not to take this deal and try to make it. Glenn you are good enough to play Big 10 basketball." He accepted the Wisconsin offer, and was officially enrolled at the University of Wisconsin with classes starting in two weeks. He then had to make the painful phone call to tell the Cornell coach that he had changed his mind and was not enrolling at Cornell and was going to Wisconsin. Here is the wording of the acceptance letter sent to Glenn on September 8, 1954.

Dear Mr. Borland

Your application for admission to the University of Wisconsin in the semester beginning September 13, is approved so late that we are using this special procedure to notify you. Please call for your New Student Week Program Monday morning, September 13 at 8:00 a.m. in Room 181 in this building.

Very Truly Yours,
Paul L. Trump
Director of Admissions

Glenn's parents got in the borrowed car and made their second three-hour journey from Oelwein to Madison, this time to drop off their one and only son, whom they had adopted just eighteen years earlier. As Glenn said goodbye to his parents, I often wonder if he was scared, lonely, and feeling the pressure of only a one year scholarship. For how could he have known on that day that he would spend the rest of his life in Madison, Wisconsin?

Glenn and his parents make one last visit to Madison. They were impressed with the lakes that surround the beautiful campus.

Coached by Jack Darland, this team went 27-1. My dad is number 33.
Photo courtesy of the Oelwein Daily Register

Glenn taking an important phone call. On the other end is Wisconsin Badger's coach Bud Foster offering Glenn a scholarship.

**Miss Nicholson**

Mr. and Mrs. Glenn Nicholson, Maynard, announce the engagement of their daughter, Carolyn, to Glenn F. Borland jr., son of Mr. and Mrs. Glenn Borland sr. of Oelwein.

Photo courtesy of the Oelwein Daily Register

## Gem D: ROMANCE

At some point in her high school days, Carolyn Nicholson heard of a high-scoring star on the boys' basketball team at Oelwein High School. And at some point in his high school days, Glenn Borland became aware that in nearby Maynard lived the talented Nicholson sisters, one of whom was a cute blond named Carolyn.

So they were aware of each other eight miles apart. Glenn was 18 during the summer between his senior year of high school and his freshman year of college. Carolyn, at age 16, between her junior and senior years of high school. That summer, they happened to be at the same softball game. They met, and the game was on. Soon after that Carolyn's sister, Betty, lobbied Glenn to ask Carolyn out, and when he said he would, Betty then worked Carolyn. "Glennie Borland is going to ask you out," she told Carolyn. "And you better say yes."

They started dating. Their relationship thrived on their mutual interests, which of course included basketball. Glenn was working as a roofer on a job along the highway between Maynard and Oelwein. Betty had a driver's license, so, time after time, she would drive Carolyn past Glenn's job site for a honk and a wave. Betty and Carolyn would drive by "a hundred times," Glenn claims. Maybe it was more like six or eight.

In fact, the day of the family barbecue, the day he threw the papers about his adoption and his birth parents into the fire, Glenn's date was Carolyn. And when Glenn's dad gave the packet of papers to Glenn, Glenn handed them off, without looking at them, to Carolyn. She glanced at them briefly and didn't have them long before Glenn grabbed them back and hurled them into the flames. But she did have them long enough to see what his birth name was: Harold Imhoff.

They dated some more and some more. All that dating eventually led to a marriage that lasted more than a half century.

Photo courtesy of the University of
Wisconsin Athletic Department

Welcome to the Wisconsin Badgers.  Photo courtesy of
the University of Wisconsin Athletic Department

## CHAPTER 7
## NINTH-BEST FRESHMAN FORWARD?

Glenn found his Madison apartment and was given the class schedule the school had set up for him. The next day he would be enrolled at the University of Wisconsin with his one-year guaranteed scholarship.

In the 1950s, the University of Wisconsin was in many ways the same as it is today. It was a big state research university whose reputation was a rare combination of elements: The school was and is considered an intellectual heavyweight with a distinguished faculty, but at the same time it was and is known to be a roaring, freewheeling party school. The university had (and continues to have) a stellar academic reputation and is one of the most respected universities in the country. The student body has long been diverse, including kids from Wisconsin farms and small towns, students from such big Midwestern cities as Chicago, Milwaukee, and Minneapolis; and serious students from the East Coast who could have been accepted at Ivy League schools.

There weren't a lot of dormitories at the University of Wisconsin. Students beyond their freshman year, and even many freshmen, drifted into off-campus housing, which was scattered throughout downtown Madison and its fringes. The luckier students found nice, well-furnished digs. Others ended up in rat holes. Student rentals were big business in Madison, and many landlords jammed too many students into a property. In the '50s and for years after some students actually lived in closets or on porches. Glenn Borland lived on a porch. And he shared that porch with two other University of Wisconsin basketball players. Calling Glenn's living space an apartment was a stretch. Incredibly, the porch was not heated. In the winter, the landlord would heat up bricks and put them in blankets all around the porch to help keep the guys warm.

With his mom and dad back in Iowa and his girlfriend Carolyn still in high school, Glenn was on his own for the first time in his life. A kid from a small town in Iowa with a lot of basketball talent was thrust into what seemed like a big city, and had to excel at basketball to keep his scholarship.

In those days college freshman were not allowed to play on the varsity. The freshmen formed a separate team. Glenn was scared and homesick on the first day of practice as Fritz Wegner, the freshman coach, welcomed his new team to the University of Wisconsin basketball program.

At the end of the first practice day, Glenn was shocked to learn that he was rated as the ninth forward on the freshman team and was surrounded by former all-state players from Wisconsin and Minnesota. Ninth-rated freshman forwards were not expected to make the varsity, so it looked like Glenn's one-year scholarship was to be short-lived,

As usual Glenn worked hard and did his best. It was discouraging for Glenn because he didn't know any of the other players and no one knew who he was or where he came from. Homesick and lonely, he went back to Oelwein seriously thinking about quitting the team, dropping out of school and moving back to Iowa. He also thought about transferring to his original choice, tiny Cornell College.

In Oelwein, he had a heart to heart talk with Jack Darland, his high school basketball coach, and they discussed the possibility of Glenn quitting the Wisconsin basketball team and dropping out of school. Darland assured Glenn that no one would blame him for coming back to Iowa. He asked Glenn one simple question: "Are those eight players that are listed ahead of you better than you?"

Dad's response was "No way. I am better than all those guys."

So his former coach responded, "Why would you quit?" As it turns out that was, the greatest advice Glenn could have gotten.

The Ninth Rated Freshman Forward headed back to Madison with a new outlook. A few weeks later the freshman team played its annual Red vs. White freshman intra-squad game. The teams were set up to be evenly matched, and expectations were high for the all the freshman to sparkle in a sort-of real game. Glenn was part of the Red team, which won a close game. Walter Holt had 23 points and Glenn Borland had 18.

The freshman team also got to play a game against the varsity, another annual event. The freshman started John Pamerin and Bob Litzow as the forwards, Steve Radke, at center, Dave Leichtfoss and Walter Holt at the guards. Those five starters were held to only 8 points against the varsity, however the Capitol Times reporter stated that "For the jittery freshman 5 Glenn Borland and John Demerit were high scorers with 10 points each, actually only Borland and Demerit turned in any classy performance for the first-year squad."

Toward the end of his first season on a cold winter night, Glenn, still feeling lonely, found himself walking through a blizzard on his way to basketball practice. He was simultaneously fighting through the snowstorm and wondering if he had played well enough to make the team. A car pulled up next to him and honked.

Glenn looked up and could barely see the car through the swirling snow. He went over to the car, and while a window was being rolled down, he noticed Iowa plates on the car.

"Where are you going?" the driver asked.

"I'm on my way to basketball practice at the field house," Glenn replied.

"Hop in," said the driver, "That's where I'm going. My name is Earl Edwards and I'm captain of the wrestling team." Dad jumped in the car, introduced himself, mentioned noticing the Iowa plates and told Edwards that he was a fellow Iowan. On that snowy ride to the field house, for the first time since arriving in Madison, Glenn felt comfortable.

Earl Edwards and Glenn would become close friends. Glenn would always jump at the chance to ride back to Iowa with Earl to spend time with his parents. However the main reason Glenn was so eager to make the long trip was to see the love of his life, Carolyn. Earl and Glenn would make dozens of trips together from Madison to Iowa. Their friendship would grow through the years, and they are still friends today.

At the end of Glenn's freshman year, the coaches posted the "invite list," which named only six freshmen who would be invited to the first day of varsity practice the next season. Glenn's name was on that list.

Glenn was thrilled. He had secured his full scholarship and was a member of the Badger basketball team.

Early in his sophomore season, Glenn moved to Number Two on the sophomore forward depth chart. Number One was Bob Litzow, and he and Glenn moved out of that porch/apartment and shared a real apartment.

In December of Glenn's sophomore season, the Badgers were scheduled to make a major West Coast trip that involved games against Stanford, Washington, Utah, and others. Only twelve of the fifteen players on the UW roster would be chosen to take the trip. Some newspaper articles raised the question of whether any sophomores would make the traveling team. The Oelwein Daily Register ran an article with the headline "Borland on Badger Traveling Squad?" If any sophomores did make it, it would be a big deal.

Glenn thought he had chance but needed a statement game. One week before the team was scheduled to leave on its West Coast trip, Glenn got his chance in a game against Nebraska. At halftime, the Badgers were down 33-27. Glenn and Bob Litzow were credited for a second half surge that spurred Wisconsin to a 71-52 victory over the Huskers. Glenn had scored 14 points in that game, with 6 points coming off his hook shot and 10 rebounds. The headline in the Capitol Times read: "Litzow Borland Are Stars." The Oelwein Daily Register's headline was "Borland hits 14; Sparks Badger Victory Surge." Other headlines from around Wisconsin and Iowa included "Borland Rallies Badgers," (Waterloo Courier) "Oelwein's Borland Stars for Badgers."(Cedar Rapids Gazette)

Bud Foster was quoted in the Milwaukee Sentinel saying, "There is no question Borland provided the spark." Foster also said, "He took over as the leader. He had a lot of hustle and it was infectious to the rest of the team."

When the traveling team was announced, Bob Litzow and Glenn were among the twelve. Glenn credits his performance against Nebraska for solidifying his position. Then Glenn was told not only did he make the traveling team, his play earned him a spot in the starting line-up. That was heady news for a sophomore who just one year before didn't look like he would make the team. The Milwaukee Journal ran a headline: "Hope Brightened: Badgers Show New Life With Borland."

The Oelwein Daily Register reported that "Oelwein's Glenn Borland will celebrate his birthday on the West Coast as a member of the Badger traveling squad." His birthday is December 28.

The weekend before they left for the West Coast, Glenn was back in Oelwein with family and friends. They decided to go to the local high school and play a pick-up basketball game like in the good old days. In that pick-up game Dad severely turned his ankle. The swelling was so bad his shoe wouldn't fit, and he could barely walk. The coach let him accompany the team on the Western trip anyway, but, as Glenn feared, he was unable to play in most of the games.

From that point on during Glenn's sophomore year he never fully recovered from his ankle injury. So he had an up and down sophomore season, well below his expectations. He did however continue to play through his injury, always guarding the opponent's toughest player. During the Big Ten season, Bud Foster was quoted as saying, "Glenn probably faced five of the toughest men in the Big Ten this year. Glenn always drew the toughest defensive assignment."

The Badgers as a team really struggled, finishing with a disappointing 6-16 record. He often wondered what would have happened if he hadn't played in that pick-up basketball game and was able to start and succeed on that West Coast trip. The disappointment of his sophomore year would motivate him to work harder and prepare for his junior season as one of the best players on the Badger team.

VIRGINIA HENNIGES, starting forward. The youngest Maynard starter as a 14-year-old freshman. At 5-8 she has developed into a great scoring threat in late season to give the Blue Devils a three pronged offense. Scored 385 points for a 13.2 average during the season. She took the spotlight by hitting 24 points in a regular season win over Monona and 25 points in the district finals to spark the Maynard win over Colesburg.

MARLENE BECKER, starting guard. One of three seniors on the Maynard squad she alternated at forward and guard a year ago before moving into the backcourt full time this season. 'Snooky' at 5-5 and 18 years old rates among the best guards in Iowa. A tremendous rebounder she joins with Dorothy Fish in patroling the front line in the Maynard defense. She is a four year veteran on the Maynard squad.

Photo courtesy of the Oelwein Daily Register    Photo courtesy of the Oelwein Daily Register

## CHAPTER 8
## TO BREAK THE PATTERN

It was a dose of déjà vu for the Maynard girls: a new season with high hopes, great expectations, and a bevy of talented returning starters. The 1955-'56 season certainly looked like yet another one of those promising years for Maynard.

But one pattern the veteran players on the Maynard team did not want to repeat was to have an outstanding regular season only to get knocked out just short of making it to the State Tournament in Des Moines. That had happened for the last three years. Each time, Maynard had torn through its regular-season competition, skated through the sectionals, won the first of two district tournament games, and then was eliminated in the district championship game. For the three Maynard senior stars, this would be their last chance.

The returning players were still feeling the pain of the previous year's loss in the district championship game. Maybe that pain would be a motivator. Or maybe it would send them on a downer that would plunge the team into mediocrity.

Carolyn was a senior now, the leader and team captain. As a junior, she had been voted third team all-state. This year she was a preseason first team selection. Glenda, her talented "little sister," wasn't so little. She had grown five inches from her sophomore to junior year and was now 5'11" to Carolyn's 5'4". With the two Nicholson sisters coming back, Coach Kupferschmid thought he just might have the scoring power he needed to compete for a state title.

Maynard also had a strong defense returning, led by future all-state guard Dorothy Fish. Also returning was the tall, physical defensive stopper junior Dorothy Fettkether.

Kupferschmid's two biggest concerns going into the season were finding a third forward to play with the Nicholsons and finding depth on the defense. He made what turned out to be a brilliant decision: He moved Carolyn's best friend, senior Marlene "Snooky" Becker, from forward/offense to guard/defense. Snooky had played offense for the past three seasons and was a key contributor. Kupferschmid decided Snooky, who was exceptionally quick, would be more valuable to the team if she switched to defense. The experience she gained playing offense, specifically her ball handling skills, would prove to be a great asset to the Maynard team later in the year. That coaching move solidified the defense as one of the best in the state.

Maynard also had several freshmen that Kupferschmid was hoping could help this talented team.

In the first month of practice, he found two surprises among his younger players. One was Mary Ann Roquet, a sophomore who would play an important role on defense as the season went on. The other was freshman Virginia Henniges. Under the guidance of Carolyn and Glenda, Virginia ended up being just what the Maynard team needed to complement the high scoring Nicholson sisters.

Virginia was a relatively unknown player to the Maynard team. She was a farm girl who grew up two miles north of Maynard. All the Maynard players were farm girls except Snooky Becker. Snooky remembers always being kidded about being the only "city" girl on the team.

Everyone called Marlene Becker Snooky. Why Snooky? She explained to me that her dad was a truck driver. While his buddies would fix the trucks, little Marlene would always watch them work. The radio show that was always on was "The Baby Snooks Show." That show starred Fanny Brice, a major Broadway actress and singer, who played Snooks, an impish 4-year-old girl who got into a lot of trouble. From that point on, Marlene Becker was known to all as Snooky.

With the 1955-'56 season about to start, Maynard's team was set. The starting lineup was:

Carolyn Nicholson, out-forward, senior, 5'4"
Glenda Nicholson, forward, junior, 5'11"
Virginia Henniges, forward, freshman, 5'8"
Marlene "Snooky" Becker, guard, senior, 5'5"
Dorothy Fish, guard, senior 5'3"
Dorothy Fettkether, guard, junior, 5'8"

The rest of the team included:

    Mary Ann Roquet, guard, sophomore 5'7"

    Lois Arthur, guard, junior, 5'11"

    Sandra Potratz, forward, freshman, 5'5"

    Barbara Fish, forward, freshman, 5'5"

    Janice Hoehne, guard, freshman, 5'6"

    Donna Turner, guard, freshman, 5'2"

Also involved were:

    Irene Harrington, team chaperone

    Jean Meyer, cheerleader

    Deanna Franklin, cheerleader

    Eleanor Holmes, cheerleader

    Janice Meyer, cheerleader

    Lois Ingels team manager

    Ann Backman, team manager

Kupferschmid was taking steps aimed at having a block-buster season.

For example, he went out of his way to schedule the toughest teams in the area. He believed that, win or lose, playing good teams would help the team later in the year and would make it tournament tough.

His practices were designed to get the maximum benefit from these short after-school hours. He never allowed first team players to scrimmage against other first team players; he wouldn't let his first team offense play against the first team defense. Coach Kupferschmid always wanted the starters to play together.

He recently told me that in one scrimmage the final score was 90-20. He said all the girls that played on the second team, most of them younger players, were upset about having to take such a shellacking. They didn't understand why the teams weren't set up to be evenly matched to make the scrimmages "fair." But Kupferschmid had his reasons. He not only wanted the first team clicking as a unit and on all cylinders going into the season, he also was preparing the younger girls for the next two to three years. The six Maynard starters that those younger girls scrimmaged against would be the toughest competition they would face at any time in their high school careers.

Barb Fish was one of those freshman players who had to struggle against the starters. She recently told me that Carolyn was the quickest girl she ever saw. "I could never stop her in practice," she said. Barb also acknowledged that playing against the first team, including her older sister Dorothy, was a great experience. Barb also said, "We never faced a better team than our own teammates in 1956 in my four year career."

Arlene Thompson was a young teacher whose first school year at Maynard was 1955-'56. Arlene came from Illinois, a state that did not allow girls to play basketball in the 1950s. She remembers watching the Maynard girls practice from the balcony, and she was "amazed" at how good those girls were. "Those girls," she thought, "are as good as the boys." She also remembers watching the Maynard girls scrimmage against the Maynard boys, as Kupferschmid was always looking for the best competition he could find.

Maynard was now ready for the first game of the 1955-'56 season. And that first game would be against Monona, the team that had delivered the heartbreaking defeat of Maynard in the district championship game the previous year.

Monona was rumored to be even stronger this year. Jean Overbeck, the Monona star, was back for her final year.

But Maynard came out on fire and won the rematch 97-68. That set the tone for the entire year. Maynard then went on to reel off fifteen straight victories. And they were blowing teams out, winning by 30, 40, and 50 points. The closest game they had in that stretch was against Garrison, and they won that one by 12. This success prompted several newspaper articles to be written about the Maynard team. The articles praised the skill of the players, commenting on the experience of the Fish and Nicholson sisters and the team's determination to win. In fact, several experts saw Maynard as one of the favorites to win the state title.

Maynard was on a tear. The Nicholsons were unstop-pable, Carolyn was averaging 31 points a game, Glenda, 34, and freshman Virginia Henniges 13. The defense was playing exceptionally well, too.

Maynard had a record of 16-0 going into a game against Grafton, a town about 20 miles from the Minnesota line that was even smaller than Maynard. Coach Koop specifically added Grafton to the schedule because of its reputation for strong teams. That year's team certainly lived up to that billing. Maynard lost a hard-fought game to Grafton 60-58. Carolyn played perhaps her worst game of the year with her boyfriend Glenn Borland in the stands watching. Grafton took a page out of the old Garnavillo playbook and used an extremely physical style to make Maynard uncomfortable, and it paid off.

After the loss, the girls expected Coach Kupferschmid to be upset. To their surprise he was calm, upbeat and, as always, positive. The girls were relieved at his positivity, and later noted that this was part of his plan to prepare them for a state tournament run. The painful loss would serve as a lesson and motivation for the girls for the rest of the season.

I recently asked Snooky Becker about Coach Kupferschmid, and she immediately confirmed my mom's feelings about their coach. "We all loved to play for Coach Kupferschmid," she said, "We all wanted to please him. We all wanted to win for him."

Mary Ann Roquet said in four years she never saw Kupferschmid get angry or yell. He never even raised his voice. He was always positive with the team, which included the chaperone, the cheerleaders and the team managers. To Kupferschmid, "the team" meant more than just the players; it meant everyone who was involved.

Jean Meyer, one of the cheerleaders, told me Coach Kupferschmid assigned her to be in charge of crowd control. Jean said he didn't want any booing or unruly fans. One poem about rude spectators at girls' basketball games, whose author is unknown, resonates with me. It goes like this:

> Please don't curse the girl down there, she's my daughter you see. She's only just a girl you know, and means a lot to me. I did not raise my daughter, sports fans, for you to call her names. She may not be a superstar, but it's

just a high school game. [14]

Fortunately, the Maynard girls didn't encounter a lot of name-calling spectators.

Jean Meyer also told me the cheerleaders sold game tickets, escorted the team onto the court before the game, and even washed some of the girls' hair. The girls were concerned about looking good when they played.

Kupferschmid put a lot of stock in team chemistry, and he gave Carolyn a lot of the credit, as the team leader and captain, for bringing the team together. Carolyn apparently went out of her way to make sure the freshmen felt welcome with the seniors. "She was a great leader, you could always count on Carolyn to come through," he said. Referring to her ability to get the team playing up to par, he called Carolyn "the straw that stirred the drink."

When I asked him what it was like to coach the Nicholson girls, he said, "They were a piece of cake, never any trouble. They always respected their coach." That came from being raised by Glenn Nicholson, for whom respect was very important.

Kupferschmid went on to say, "I loved the entire Nicholson family, a very likeable family." He loved and respected them so much, in fact, that he and his wife, Grace Ann, named one of their daughters Carolyn, after my mom. Hearing that was a very emotional experience for me. What a tribute. Like so much of this story my mom had never told me about that.

Snooky told me that Carolyn was "the real leader and was the reason the entire team was so close."

My mom was apparently very demanding, which came as no surprise to me. During practice, if the coach said shoot ten times, Carolyn would demand that the girls shoot twenty times. According to Snooky, "She went above and beyond, always one more time, until the team got it right."

After the tough loss to Grafton, Maynard won its next game 100-55. They were on fire again, winning their next six

---

14 McElwain, Max. The Only Dance In Iowa. A History of Six-Player Girls Basketball: Page 190

games and heading into the sectionals with a record of 23-1.

Coach Kupferschmid knew this team was different. They were focused, businesslike, with no big celebrations. Just a team determined to win.

As I continued to review the scores of that season's games, I kept asking how Maynard could keep winning by such big margins. Every person I asked had the same answer: We just expected to win and win big. I finally asked Coach Kupferschmid what he thought about some of these scores. He also said, "We fully expected not only to win but win big. It was almost unbelievable how good we were. We mauled the bigger schools."

But the big question that year was: Could they maul their way to Des Moines?

MAYNARD

FRONT ROW: *Carolyn Nicholson, Virginia Henniges, Glenda Nicholson, Dorothy Fettkether, Marlene Becker, Dorothy Fish.*

BACK ROW: *Donna Turner, Mary Ann Roquet, Lois Arthur, Coach Mel Kupferschmid, Janice Hoehne, Barbara Fish, Sandra Potratz.*

| NUMBERS Color of Shirt | | | | |
|---|---|---|---|---|
| BLUE | WHITE | PLAYER | POSITION | YEAR IN SCHOOL |
| 21 | 20 | CAROLYN NICHOLSON | FORWARD | SENIOR |
| 23 | 22 | MARLENE BECKER | GUARD | SENIOR |
| 41 | 40 | DOROTHY FISH | GUARD | SENIOR |
| 31 | 30 | DOROTHY FETTKETHER | GUARD | JUNIOR |
| 51 | 50 | GLENDA NICHOLSON | FORWARD | JUNIOR |
| 55 | 54 | LOIS ARTHUR | GUARD | JUNIOR |
| 53 | 52 | MARY ANN ROQUET | GUARD | SOPHOMORE |
| 33 | 32 | VIRGINIA HENNIGES | FORWARD | FRESHMAN |
| 43 | 42 | SANDRA POTRATZ | FORWARD | FRESHMAN |
| 25 | 24 | BARBARA FISH | FORWARD | FRESHMAN |
| 45 | 44 | JANICE HOEHNE | GUARD | FRESHMAN |
| 35 | 34 | DONNA TURNER | GUARD | FRESHMAN |

County: Fayette

Superintendent: William A. Tock      Coach: Melvin Kupferschmid
High School Enrollment: 141           Population of Town: 452
School Colors: Blue and White        Team Nickname: Blue Devils

SEASON'S RECORD: Won 29, Lost 1

Photo courtesy of IGHSAU

**SAD AND DEJECTED,** the Maynard Blue Devilettes move off the floor after last Saturday night's loss to Garnavillo in the finals of the district tournament at Decorah. Visible are (left to right) Judy Buenneke, Dorothy Fish, Beverly Windenburg, Marlene Becker, Betty Nicholson and Pat Cummings. Their sorrow is made obvious by the score shown above. (Photo by West.)

## C. Nicholson Top Scorer Hits 52 Points

By ERNIE ESCHBACH
Managing Editor

An unstopable display of offensive power shoved the Maynard girls into the state district basketball contest Saturday night in sectional finals at Fayette with a 86-64 victory over the strong Ossian DeSales club.

A steady stream of 30 first quarter points engulfed the DeSales girls before they could set their sights on the basket or make their defense function properly.

Spearheading the attack for Maynard was Carolyn Nicholson, a smooth, tricky, hard-driving forward who poured in 20 of the 30 first quarter points and accounted for 52 points for the game.

The victory wasn't a one girl show, though. Post forward Glenda Nicholson, showing a future promise with a good hook shot, took up where her sister left off, tossing 29 points through the hoop.

Box Score:

| MAYNARD (86) | Fg | Ft | F | Tp |
|---|---|---|---|---|
| Nicholson, C | 18 | 16 | 2 | 52 |
| Nicholson, G | 11 | 7 | 2 | 29 |
| Hennigs | 1 | 0 | 0 | 2 |
| DeLong | 1 | 1 | 1 | 3 |
| Becker | 0 | 0 | 5 | 0 |
| Windenburg | 0 | 0 | 3 | 0 |
| Fish | 0 | 0 | 4 | 0 |
| Feitkeiher | 0 | 0 | 3 | 0 |
| Totals | 31 | 24 | 19 | 86 |
| DESALES (64) | | | | |
| Murphy | 16 | 12 | 0 | 44 |
| Brom | 2 | 4 | 2 | 8 |
| Klisart | 3 | 5 | 2 | 11 |
| Figge | 0 | 0 | 5 | 0 |
| Rohr | 0 | 0 | 1 | 0 |
| Rohr, A | 0 | 0 | 2 | 0 |
| Giblin | 0 | 0 | 3 | 0 |
| Totals | 21 | 22 | 16 | 64 |

Score by Quarters:

| | | | | |
|---|---|---|---|---|
| Ossian | 13 | 16 | 21 | 14—64 |
| Maynard | 30 | 18 | 20 | 20—86 |

The seniors still had bad memories of the previous district finals.

Years ago my mom casually mentioned to me she scored 52 points in a high school game as a junior. It would take me seven years, but I did find the proof.

Photo courtesy of the Oelwein Daily Register

My dad's tiny house in Oelwein, Iowa.

### Gem E: PERSONA NON GRATA

Heading into the 1956 sectional, the Maynard team was full of confidence and was playing great basketball. Coach Kupferschmid made a special request.

In 1956 Carolyn was dating Glenn Borland, who was going to college in Madison, Wisconsin, and playing basketball for the Wisconsin Badgers.

Glenn would often visit his family and friends in Oelwein, Iowa, which was eight miles from Maynard, and on such visits he would get together with Carolyn. Glenn attended Maynard's regular-season Grafton game, which turned out to be the only game that the Maynard girls lost all season. And that night Carolyn played her worst game of the year.

Coach Kupferschmid asked Glenn Nicholson to ask Glenn Borland not to come to any more games because his daughter, Carolyn, got too nervous when her Big Ten basketball playing boyfriend was watching.

I can picture my mom looking into the stands for my dad during the game. It makes me laugh and cry at the same time.

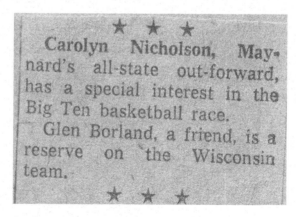

★ ★ ★
Carolyn Nicholson, Maynard's all-state out-forward, has a special interest in the Big Ten basketball race.
Glen Borland, a friend, is a reserve on the Wisconsin team.
★ ★ ★

Credit: Des Moines Register

GLENDA NICHOLSON, starting post forward. The greatest single season scorer in Maynard history she needs only two points in the state tournament to top the 1,000 point mark for one season. At 5-10 the 16-year-old junior stands as one of the most improved players on the Maynard squad. Her high points for the season were 52 against Waucoma in the county and 51 in the Blue Devils win over Aurora, queens of Buchanan coun-... A definite all-state candi-

Courtesy of Oelwein Daily Register

CAROLYN NICHOLSON, starting forward. The greatest scorer in all Maynard girls' basketball history. An 18-year-old, 5-4, senior she is captain of the Blue Devils. She has 903 points as the quarterback of the Maynard offense. Set a career mark for Iowa outforwards with 2,978 points. Hit over 40 points in four games this season. Started on four straight Maynard county championship teams. A third team all-state selection a year ago she is virtually a cinch for more honors this season.

Courtesy of Oelwein Daily Register

## CHAPTER 9
## SECTIONAL TIME

As the Maynard team boarded the bus to head to its first 1956 sectional game, Snooky Becker was thinking about all the long, dreary bus trips they had taken throughout the season. Most of the buses had cold, uncomfortable seats and no heat. The players, cheerleaders, and others would sing songs and make up games to pass the time.

Snooky recalls that Coach Kupferschmid would always sit in the middle of the bus with the girls to build relationships between coach and players. He made sure the freshman sat with the seniors and that the cheerleaders were mixed in with the players. Kupferschmid knew that chemistry would be key with this team, and that without it, Maynard might come up short again, in spite of their obvious talent. He also knew that it was entirely possible that even the youngest players on the team might be called upon at some point to make key contributions in big moments. Events would prove the wisdom of his strategy, as the team, with the help of its leader Carolyn Nicholson, developed a close bond, such that even the freshman players felt they were an important part of the team.

Most of the towns they would travel to had small gyms with outdated facilities. Most of the gyms did not have hot water, so the girls couldn't shower after those games. In fact most locker rooms didn't even have running water. The tiny Maynard gym had just one locker room, so the home team, Maynard, would always let the visiting team use that locker room. The Maynard girls would use Ms. Harrington's third grade home room as their locker room.

As they had in the three previous sectionals, Maynard dominated its opponents, winning the three sectional games 102-50, 92-37, and 89-36, outscoring their opponents 283-123, for a whopping 53-point average margin of victory.

Maynard was in the now familiar position of needing just two more wins to go to the State Tournament. Their first opponent in district play was Monona. Once again they would have to deal with Jean Overbeck. Revenge-minded Maynard had beaten Monona soundly in the season opener, avenging the defeat in the district final game the previous year, so Maynard was favored. But Maynard had been favored to beat Monona the previous year. Would Monona again pull the upset? The winner would get to play 30-0 Colesburg, and the winner of that game would go to the State Tournament.

According to the 1956 Maynard yearbook, Maynard's record was 119-14 the previous five seasons with zero trips to the State Tournament. Coach Kupferschmid said that in those district final games that Maynard lost —to Garnavillo twice and to Monona — "The guards collapsed," implying that the team couldn't make it to the State Tournament because the defense couldn't handle the pressure of the district finals. Maybe that's why he moved the talented Snooky Becker to defense.

This time no part of the Maynard team collapsed. All of their offseason work paid off as Maynard left no doubt, beating Monona 83-64. The Nicholson girls' total of 63 points was one shy of Monona's entire team. As Jack Ogden reported in the Des Moines Register:

> The talented Maynard girls completely overpowered Monona here Thursday night to move into Saturday's district final against undefeated Colesburg.
>
> Hitting 64% of its shots, Maynard piled up a better than 30 point lead before sending in the subs and winding up with a convincing 83-64 victory.
>
> The Nicholson sisters, Carolyn and Glenda, again were the scoring standouts in Maynard's semifinal victory, but it was a magnificent team effort that provided the third victory of the year over a Monona club that made it to the State finals a year ago.

He later wrote:

> Carolyn, already the all-time Iowa scoring champion for an out-forward, tossed in 31 points with an assortment

of shots while sister Glenda contributed 32.

Maynard's other starting forward, Virginia Henniges, popped in 7 baskets for 14 points.

Colesburg looked to be a tough opponent in the district championship game. Any team that's undefeated in 30 games should get the attention of an opposing team. And there was that seeming district-final jinx that had been haunting Maynard.

Jack Ogden continued:

> Saturday the once beaten Fayette County queens and the unbeaten Delaware County and Upper Mississippi champs tangle in the tourney feature at 8:30.

Maynard became a ghost town the day of the game. Most if not all of the 455 residents traveled to Garnavillo in hope of seeing their team earn a State Tournament berth, and 1,500 fans packed into the small Garnavillo gym for what promised to be a thrilling game.

Maynard was unstoppable, and Colesburg turned out to be no match for the high-flying Maynard girls, who won 76-49. Freshman Virginia Henniges played her best game of the year, scoring 25 points. Carolyn had 29 points and Glenda scored 22. Toward the end of the game, the crowd was chanting "Des Moines, Des Moines." Barb Fish, a freshman in 1956, recently said, "I remember those chants like it was yesterday."

An article by John Meyer in the Oelwein Daily Register said:

> "Six years of rebuilding since the sport was rejuvenated in Maynard in 1950 was climaxed at Garnavillo Saturday night when a standing room only crowd of 1,500 saw the Blue Devils formally sway the Northeast Iowa balance of power to Maynard with a comparatively easy 76-49 win over Colesburg in the District Tournament Finals."

Coach Kupferschmid, now 28-1, had the best season record in the history of Maynard basketball. The State Tournament team of 1924 was 23-1, but lost in the first State Tournament game 20-14. The pressure of getting to the State Tournament was finally lifted from Carolyn and the rest of the Maynard team. With their backs now monkey-free, they were excited, nervous, and ready to start preparing for an opportunity of a lifetime.

There would be no shortage of running water or locker rooms in their next venue, Veterans Memorial Auditorium in Des Moines, which would seat 15,000 people — more than thirty times the population of Maynard.

**Russ Smith's Column ‑ ‑**

## Fish, Nicholson Girls' Combined Talents Place Maynard Among State Tournament Favorites

THERE'S BEEN AT LEAST one member each from the Fish and Nicholson families on the Maynard High girls' basketball team since the sport was installed in the school program in 1951.

This year there are two members of each family on the squad and the Fayette county champions who never have had a losing season, are bound for the state tournament for the first time in history.

Both of the Nicholsons are candidates to succeed their sister, Betty, as all-state performers. Carolyn, the senior, owns a record point total as an out-

forward—2,975 so far in four years.

Glenda, her "big" sister who is a junior, plays the post forward and has outscored Carolyn 998-905 so far this season. Glenda's average for 29 games has been 34.1 and Carolyn's 31.1.

Dorothy Fish, one of three seniors on the squad, is a starting guard. Her sister, Barbara, a freshman, also is a member of the state tournament squad. Glenda is the last of the basketball playing Nicholsons. Brother Jim is a member this season of the Blue Devils' new-

ly-organized wrestling squad. Dorothy Fish and Glenda Nicholson both are straight A students in school.

Other starters on Coach Mel Kupferschmidt's team are forward Virginia Hennigs, a freshman, and guards Marlene Becker, a senior, and Dorothy Fettkether, a junior.

Although Maynard's population, according to the 1950 census, was only 455, the

school is comfortably into the class A bracket with a five-year average daily attendance of 140.07. Becker is the only town girl in the starting lineup. The other five are from neighboring farms.

Kupferschmidt plans to take his squad to Des Moines Monday and get it established in its tournament residence, the Kirkwood Hotel. The team will take advantage of its assigned 40-minute practice period at the Veterans' Memorial Auditorium.

*Courier*

WATERLOO, IOWA, SATURDAY, FEBRUARY 25, 1956

THE MAYNARD GIRLS' had no trouble packing their suit cases into three cars Monday morning for the trip to Des Moines. Here are five starters, Carolyn and Glenda Nicholson, Dorothy Fish, Dorothy Fettkether and Marlene Becker as part of the Maynard student body helped load in the suit cases. A pep rally and parade trip through town marked the start of the trip. (Register Photo.)

Courtesy of Oelwein Daily Register

The girls ironing their new uniforms. From left: Glenda Nicholson, Carolyn Nicholson, Virginia Henniges and Dorothy Fettkether
Photo courtesy of Cedar Rapids Gazette

## CHAPTER 10
## THE BIG TIME

All 455 residents of Maynard were making plans to go to Des Moines. People from neighboring towns, thousands of them, were also planning their trip to Des Moines. The Maynard girls had no idea how popular they had become.

Earl Foss, the mayor of Maynard, said it was Maynard's time, and he invited all the residents to make the trip. The excitement was building for the Maynard team to start its journey to Des Moines.

I asked my mom if she remembers what her thoughts were. That question triggered a collage of memories. Mom immediately harkened back to the incredible effort her father put forward to get a Maynard girls' team. Carolyn understood how fortunate she was to have the opportunity to play.

Mom also reflected on how lucky the Nicholsons were to have the Fish family move into the area. Without the addition of the Fish girls, Maynard might not have gotten a team. Her thoughts also went back to the 1950-'51 season when her oldest sister Lou Ann helped get the Maynard program off the ground. She also felt bad for her sister Betty, who was such a great player but never got the opportunity to play in the State Tournament. She was very grateful to her two older sisters for laying the groundwork for the Maynard program.

Barb Fish, like Carolyn, credits her older sisters for setting the stage for Maynard's impressive run. Barb felt fortunate to get to experience the State Tournament with her sister Dorothy, but she "felt bad for Marjorie that she never got a chance to play in the State Tournament."

The Fish and Nicholson girls were truly something special. Several articles appeared in newspapers all over the area talking about them. One article, a piece by Russ Smith of the Waterloo Courier on Saturday February 25th 1956 read in part:

"Fish, Nicholson Girls Combined Talents Place Maynard among State Tournament Favorites.

There's been at least one member each from the Fish and Nicholson families on the Maynard High Girls Basketball

Team since the sport was installed in the school program in 1951."

"This year there are two members of each family on the squad."

"Both of the Nicholsons are candidates to succeed their sister, Betty, as all-state performers. Carolyn, the senior, owns a record point total as an out forward - 2,978 so far in four years.

Glenda, her 'big' sister is a junior, plays the post forward and has outscored Carolyn 998-903 so far this season. Glenda's average for 29 games has been 34.1 and Carolyn's 31.1.

Dorothy Fish, one of three seniors on the squad, is a starting guard. Her sister, Barbara, a freshman, also is a member of the state tournament squad."

There had never been a basketball team at Maynard without a Nicholson or Fish since the program's resurrection six years before.

On February 28, 1956, a group of Maynard students helped the girls load their suitcases into three cars for the two and a half hour trip to Des Moines.

Before they left, the girls had to cope with an unexpected bout of nervousness.

After the district championship game, the town of Maynard made the collective decision that the teams' uniforms were old and on the drab side. The Maynard Booster Club had suggested that the team deserved better uniforms, so it was decided to get new, livelier ones. The budget was set at $500. The uniforms were ordered. They were to be blue and white satin, two piece with jackets featuring the torso hip-line and pleats. The fancy blue uniforms would end up costing $750. The Maynard Bank contributed $250 to make up for the difference.

Two days before they were to leave, the uniforms had not arrived. All the girls were worried that they wouldn't get to wear them. Snooky remembers all the girls "were measured and fitted for these new gorgeous blue skirt uniforms." They were also worried that somehow the measurements were wrong and they wouldn't fit.

The new uniforms arrived the day before they were to

leave for Des Moines. The girls spent a few moments oohing and aahing over the new uniforms, then they started to wonder if the skirts would be too short or not sewn properly. Once they tried the uniforms on, they were relieved to learn that the tights were sewn in under the short skirts. They all fit, and the girls loved their flashy new uniforms.

The girls piled into three cars, new uniforms in hand, and set off. Unbeknownst to the girls, Maynard had planned a rousing sendoff for them. As they rode through town, the girls were surprised to find the streets lined with fans from all over the area. They left Maynard to a stirring pep rally and parade. The girls' caravan made it through the pep rally and parade, and they were on their way to Des Moines. That sendoff made some of the girls start to realize what a big deal it was to make the State Tournament.

Many of the players had never really been out of Maynard except to play basketball, and most had never stayed in a hotel. All of that, of course, was about to change.

In Des Moines, the team checked into the Kirkwood Hotel, just blocks from Vet's Auditorium. They arrived Monday night with their first event scheduled for Tuesday, a forty-five minute practice on the floor of Vet's Auditorium.

Once the players, managers, cheerleaders, and coaches settled into their rooms, the hallway that led to their rooms would be guarded by team chaperone, Irene Harrington. The girls still did not realize how popular they were. Hundreds of fans wanted to visit the Kirkwood Hotel to see the girls. But Coach Kupferschmid decided to sequester the girls in the Kirkwood during the entire stay. They would not even be able to see friends or family. Coach Kupferschmid wanted them to focus and did not want any distractions.

Over the five-day period hundreds and hundreds of flowers, plenty of fruit and candy, and well-wishing telegrams were delivered to the girls. That outpouring further served to awaken the Maynard farm girls to the fact that they were part of a huge event. And they were learning that most of Northeast Iowa was heading to Des Moines to support them.

Of the hundreds of telegrams the girls received while in

Des Moines, one stands out in the memory of Mary Ann Roquet. It came from Oelwein, where the high school had a boys' team but did not have a girls' team. The telegram read: "The Huskies are our boys, but Maynard you are our girls. Go Maynard and good luck!"

Irene Harrington, the team chaperone, was the Maynard third grade teacher. Glenda and Carolyn described her as "a very nice, but strict lady."

At the Kirkwood Hotel, Ms. Harrington was a diligent guard. She would sit at the end of the wing of the hotel floor, shielding the girls from their enthusiastic fans. No one could get past Irene Harrington, no matter how hard they tried.

Ms. Harrington was also in charge of the lemons. Every day, hours before the game time, she would shop for lemons, cut them up, put them in bags, and bring them to the game. She believed that water wore you down, so she made the girls suck on lemons instead of drinking water.

Her other main responsibilities were to keep the girls in line and to keep boys and the boyfriends away from the girls during the tournament. The team did not need any distractions.

It's unlikely that the girls were angelically well behaved for the entire trip. Mom never told me this story, but when I asked Snooky if the girls got into any trouble in Des Moines, she laughed and said, "Well Brian, your mom and I, when Ms. Harrington wasn't watching, we had noticed the windows did not have screens, so we would open the windows and sit on the ledge and drop water balloons down on the fans and some of the boyfriends." Looking back, Snooky said, "Yeah that was probably a little dangerous."

In 1956, the tournament field was not separated into classes or divisions as it is today. Schools of all sizes – from big cities and small towns were all in the same pool. All that mattered was how good your team was, not where you were from. 700 schools from all over the state were whittled down to the "Sweet Sixteen" – the 16 best teams who would meet in Des Moines. As one of the smallest schools in the tournament, Maynard had a daunting challenge before them.

The team's Tuesday afternoon practice at Vet's Auditorium was scheduled for forty-five minutes. The girls were shocked and in awe at how big Vet's was compared to the tiny Maynard gym. Their first and only practice was terrible. Coach Kupferschmid had never seen the girls play so badly, so he was worried. The second team outplayed the first team throughout the practice. The coach really didn't know what to expect or how the girls would play. For the first time his team looked scared.

Maynard's first game was scheduled for Wednesday night against Albert City, which was the tallest team in the tournament and had a 30-1 record. The Oelwein Daily Register reported that "Kuperschmid was doubly worried. Not only was he set to face one of the tallest teams in the tournament in Albert City, but in addition his Blue Devils had a miserable practice session Tuesday afternoon...The stage fright of the giant Des Moines Auditorium apparently shook the Blue Devils." Carolyn would later confirm that, saying: "We were truly petrified."

When the disappointing first practice ended, the girls were under strict supervision and escorted back to their hotel where they had to regroup and get ready for Albert City. The game was less than twenty-four hours away. Back in their hotel they still had to do homework and iron and press their new uniforms, all under the guidance of Ms. Harrington.

When the tournament bracket was announced, the girls took note that their first opponent would be Albert City. But they couldn't help but notice something else as well: Maynard was in the same bracket as the favored Grafton team, which had a perfect 32-0 record and was the team that handed Maynard its only loss, a 2 point thriller. The girls quickly noticed that Maynard and Grafton would meet in the semifinals if they both won their first two games.

For some reason the media took a special interest in the Maynard team. Reporters were fascinated with Maynard's six year rebuilding story, their potent offense, their stingy defense, and, of course, the Nicholson sisters. Some newspapers picked Maynard as the favorite, and why not? They were thumping opponents by an average score of 86-50. Coach Kupferschmid was asked about being a favorite and his response was, "I have the Nicholson girls; we have a chance."

The media were also very interested in the Nicholson girls' point totals. No two teammates had ever scored 1,000 points each in the same season. Carolyn and Glenda were close. Going into the State Tournament, Glenda had 998 and Carolyn had 903. With a solid tournament, the sisters could make history. There was a picture in The Oelwein Daily Register before the tournament featuring Glenda and Carolyn holding a big sign that said 1,000. Carolyn was embarrassed by this; she didn't want the attention, and, like many athletes, she didn't want to be perceived as being concerned about her point totals. But she agreed to pose for the picture. The caption under the picture stated:

"Hoping for 1,000! Glenda and Carolyn Nicholson pose beside a sign carrying the figure 1,000- the goal they are shooting for as individual totals for the season. All Maynard hopes they make it too and if they do, it almost certainly would mean the Blue Devils will advance through four games in Des Moines."

On Wednesday, the new uniforms were ironed, the homework was finished, and it was game time.

Coach Kupferschmid making sure the girls did their homework. My mom told me they couldn't concentrate on their homework. Photo courtesy of The Waterloo Courier

HOPING FOR 1000! Glenda and Carolyn Nicholson pose beside a sign carrying the figure 1,000 — the goal they're shooting for as individual totals for the season. All Maynard hopes they make it too and if they do it'll almost certainly mean the Blue Devils will advance through four games in Des Moines. (Register Photo.)

Photo courtesy of the Oelwein Daily Register

DOROTHY FISH, 17-year-old senior starting guard. Smallest starter
at only 5-3 she is the girl who
stopped Monona's all-stater Jean
Overbeck, allowing the all-time
great only seven shots and two
baskets in the first half hour of
Maynard's district tournament win.
Fast and rugged she rates as one
of the finest guards in the state.
One of three seniors who will be
making their last appearance in a
Maynard uniform in the Des
Moines tournament.

DOROTHY FETTKETHER, starting post guard. 16 years old and a
junior she's the big girl in the Blue
Devil defense at 5-8. Giving up
height to almost every opponent
she has nevertheless checked the
best Northeast Iowa has had to offer including standouts such as
Darnell Walters of Colesburg,
Kathy Stevens of Fayette, Ann
Arensburg of Garrison and Arlene
Knudson of Clermont-Elgin.

Photo courtesy of the Oelwein Daily Register

Photo courtesy of the Oelwein Daily Register

## Gem F: DEFENSE, DEFENSE!

Coach Kupferschmid was proud of the fact that only twelve teams had scored over 50 points against Maynard all season long. "Our guards were very impressive," he said.

When Coach Kupferschmid explained to me how good the 1956 team's defense was, I got more intrigued with the 6 on 6 style, with three guards only playing defense and only playing in half court.

The offensive success is easier to understand, as you can monitor scoring averages, assists, etc. What was the key to the Maynard defense? In my recent conversation with Snooky, she helped put it in perspective for me.

The 1956 team defense consisted of several key players, including the three starters.

At 5'8" junior Dorothy Fettkether was Maynard's biggest defensive starter. She always had to guard the biggest and usually the most talented post player. She led the team in rebounds and blocked shots. Coach Kupferschmid said Dorothy Fettkether was a "super rebounder." Once she got the rebound she would quickly pass it to Snooky or Dorothy Fish.

The second starting guard was 5'3" senior Dorothy Fish. One of the best guards/defenders in the state, she was voted second team all-state. She was a tough, tenacious defender, very physical, also a good ball handler. She was very quick. She was a quiet person who understood her role on the team. She usually was assigned to guard the opponent's quickest player. Coach Kupferschmid described Dorothy Fish as a "fiery rushing guard."

Snooky, the 5'5" Marlene Becker, was the third starting guard/defender. Snooky, a senior, was also very quick, a great ball handler and physical. She would also help guard the top out-forward. Once they stopped their opponents from scoring, she

would quickly get the ball up to mid court and pass it to Carolyn, who was usually trying to get open at mid-court.

In their practices, they would spend hours and hours working on getting the ball from defense to offense at the half-court
line. That quick, smooth transition is very important in 6 on 6.
The key was to be quick with the ball once the defense got the
rebound. Coach Kupferschmid would always stress "Don't fool
around with the ball, get the ball to Carolyn." In carrying out
that injunction, Snooky's ball-handling skills were a huge asset
to the Maynard team.

Snooky recently recalled Coach Kupferschmid's passing drills
"We would spend hours and hours on those passing drills."
The pass or transfer was the key as all six girls needed to work
together. Coach Kupferschmid would call Snooky the "old pro...
never out of position." Marlene Becker would later join Carolyn
as a first team All-State selection.

I was beginning to understand why the Maynard defense was so
good. With two seniors both quick and good ball handlers, and
Dorothy Fettkether in the middle, it is no surprise they were so
successful. But, would they be ready for the very tall Albert City
team?

The 1956 Maynard team. Photo courtesy of IGHSAU

Snooky, Carolyn and Glenda did get out for some shopping.
Photo courtesy of the Oelwein Daily Register

Girls relaxing in their hotel room the night before the big game.
Photo courtesy of the Oelwein Daily Register

**Coach Tapes Ankle**

Keeping his girls ready for the state tournament is a fulltime job for Maynard Coach Mel Kupferschmid. Here he tapes the ankle of guard Lois Arthur while teammates in the background relax with balloons in a Des Moines hotel. (Telegraph-Herald Photos)

Photo courtesy of Dubuque Telegraph Herald

Coach Kupferschmid's last minute adjustments.
Photo courtesy of the Oelwein Daily Register

## CHAPTER 11
## CRUNCH TIME

The Maynard farm girls were now ready for the biggest moment in their young lives. And they were nervous.

Maynard played all of its State Tournament games at night and not during the day like most other teams. Snooky recently told me that, "We all wished our games were during the day because when the games were at night, we had all day to be nervous."

The press continued to be fascinated by this team and its story. Reporters even wanted to know details of the Nicholson family's daily life. Grandma Ruth had plenty of opportunity to sing her daughters' praises, including talking about their skills as farmhands. The public just couldn't get enough of the Nicholson girls, to the point that even stories about their farm-girl chores were big news.

The press had really hyped this game. A sound off by John Meyer, a girls' basketball reporter for the Oelwein Daily Register stated:

...The Blue Devils are rolling into the "Sweet Sixteen" for the first time since 1924. The successful conquest of district competition is the climax of seven (sic) years of building at the Fayette County School since the rejuvenation of the girls sport in 1951.

It took four years of district tournament play for Maynard to make the grade despite a tremendous overall mark of 126 wins against only 23 losses since the sport was reactivated...

...The Westerners should provide the same problems for Maynard that Grafton and Colesburg gave the Blue Devils on the path to the state meet.

...With three girls near the 6' mark, Albert City stands a definite challenge to any Maynard title aspirations.

Going into the game Coach Kupferschmid was very fearful of the Albert City giants. And during the National Anthem Carolyn remembers looking over at the 30-1 Albert City team and feeling intimidated by how tall they were.

But once the game started, Albert City's size and record did not matter. Maynard shook off any pre-game jitters and routed Albert City 72-44.

The papers were now all over the Maynard team.

Several articles appeared the following day. The headline from Mitch Milavetz's article in the Dubuque Telegraph-Herald read: Blue Devils Advance By Ripping Albert City

"Machine like Maynard with a meat grinder type offense and a unique "screaming" defense swamped helpless Albert City 72-44 here Wednesday"

"It was Maynard whose stock went soaring after the first round play was completed. The potent Fayette County team looked like the only polished gem in a crown field of sixteen jewels"

"It was little Carolyn Nicholson who stood out in the victory. The pint sized out-forward who ranks as Iowa's all-time great scorer from that position, proved to be a masterful quarterback besides a proficient point maker.

Her night's total was only 23 points but her spot passing set up countless goals for teammates Glenda Nicholson and Virginia Henniges"

"Glenda was high for the game with 35 while Virginia added 12.

There was no doubt about the outcome from the very start. Maynard moved out to a 4-0 lead, pushed it to 12-3 and then coasted into a 29-9 quarter margin"

"In the meantime, the backcourt combination of Snooky Becker, Dorothy Fettkether and Dorothy Fish displayed the best defensive skill of the tournament with their wild screams.

All three girls would press to close-in on shooters and flood the air with shouts of "No" "No" or "Hey" in an effort to upset the poise of their opponents"

"Fish, who is only 5'3", did a remarkable job as a post guard with Fettkether"

In his article about the game, John Meyer of the Oelwein Daily Register wrote:

Maynard Pounds Albert City 72-44

"Mel Kupferschmidt's magnificent Blue Devils rocked the Des Moines Veterans Auditorium"

"In 32 minutes all of Iowa learned what the Northeast corner of the state had known for the entire 1955-56 season. Maynard has probably the most powerful three pronged offense to offer and without a doubt the most underrated defense in the state"

"To put it bluntly Albert City was never in the ball game"

After the Albert City game there was again no big celebration. I keep going back to what the pint sized out-forward (my mom) kept telling me, "It was really no big deal. We won another game by 30 plus points. Who's next?"

Another article from the Oelwein Daily Register summed up Maynard's businesslike attitude:

"You'd never have known Maynard was in the State Tournament quarter finals Wednesday night by watching Coach Mel Kupferschmid and the Blue Devils after their comparatively easy sweep past Albert City 72-44. The Blue Devils quietly retired to the dressing room and Coach Kupferschmid went into the stands to watch Clarence and Oakland die without wild celebrations. Despite the fact that it was the first State appearance for the Maynard team, both Coach Kupferschmid and his girls had little to say and no one would believe it was the best Blue Devil victory of the season.

Kupferschmid, the 27 year old genius of the girls sport said, "our offense was great and defense even better tonight, but it wasn't our best game."

His girls were even more convinced it wasn't to be their best game. Team Captain Carolyn Nicholson, summed up their desires when she said, "our best remembered and best game we play will be when we win the state title."

Carolyn said that as she and the rest of the Maynard squad dashed off for the Kirkwood Hotel and rest for Clarence."

Carolyn was clearly confident and focused and the Maynard team was obviously over their State Tournament jitters.

Thursday

On Thursday, a focused and confident Maynard team faced Clarence.

Another game, another rout. Mitch Milavetz's headline from the Dubuque Telegraph-Herald read:

Maynard Blue Devils rout Clarence 81-44

"It was little Carolyn Nicholson who provided the offensive spark again Thursday. She tallied 32 points but that again was secondary to her scoring assists. It was her passing that set up most of sister's Glenda's 27 points and Virginia Henniges' 14"

"As an added side light to the tournament, Carolyn ran her season point total to 958 with two games left to play, giving Maynard a good chance to become the first school in girls' basketball to have two players go over 1000 in a season. Glenda now has scored 1060."

"Carolyn, by the way, has now scored 3033 points for her career. A record for an out-forward."

The Oelwein Daily Register reported: Clarence Is No Problem; Falls 81-44

"The sensational Nicholson combination caught fire immediately to tear the game wide open"

"Maynard was uncanny in the first half, hitting 18 of 22, including six straight by Carolyn Nicholson and a like number by sister Glenda"

"Coach Kupferschmid was quoted, "We made the best effort of the season tonight." and "We had the feel of the floor tonight. It was almost like playing at home in Maynard.""

Clarence Coach Jerry Gallagher called Maynard's forwards "The greatest offense in the state."

"Carolyn Nicholson, the nearest thing to greased lighting, among the tournament out-forwards, hit 32 points."

Now all of the talk around the State Tournament was the highly anticipated rematch with Grafton. Most experts believed that the winner of that game would win the State Tournament. Grafton was the only team that beat Maynard all year, so in the tournament semifinal it would be 32-0 Grafton versus 30-1 Maynard. Kupferschmid was concerned. "I don't know if we can be up two nights in a row," he said.

CAROLYN NICHOLSON, Maynard's candidate for all-state honors, decided to see how it felt to ride on a policeman's motorcycle while in Des Moines for the state girls basketball finals. (Register Photo.)

Photo courtesy of the Oelwein Daily Register

The Maynard starting lineup during the national anthem minutes before the big rematch against Grafton in front of a sold out Vets auditorium. From left to right:Carolyn Nicholson, Virginia Henniges, Glenda Nicholson, Snooky Becker, Dorothy Fettkether and Dorothy Fish.

Friday

On Friday night it was madness at Vet's Auditorium as 13,000 fans packed the gym to see the re-match of the year. By now the Maynard girls were local celebrities.

Maynard was getting a chance to avenge its only defeat of the season, a 60-58 loss to Grafton.

The Kirkwood Hotel was by Friday night littered with flowers and telegrams, hundreds and hundreds of them. The police asked my mom to ride on a police motorcycle in downtown Des Moines.

I said, "Mom you can't ride a motorcycle." She responded, "I guess when I was 18 years old I could."

It seemed like the entire population of Northeastern Iowa was in Veterans Auditorium cheering on the Blue Devils. Mayors, school superintendents and media people all wanted to be a part of the Maynard team.

My mom talks about this game probably more than any other game she has ever played in.

She remembers that the strict Irene Harrington, who never wore the Maynard blue colors, had been presented with a beautiful new blue shirt that matched the new uniforms. It was a good luck gift from the second grade class from Maynard Elementary. She wore it for the first time during the semi-finals.

Carolyn remembers the regular-season Grafton game, a tough physical game in which the potent Maynard offense was held to just 58 points, 28 points below their season average.

The mighty Grafton team, which started four seniors, had all the confidence going into the tournament semifinal game. They had earlier hit 81% of their shots in tournament play. Grafton was coming off an impressive 92-69 trouncing of New Sharon to reach the semi-final against Maynard.

Both Coach Kupferschmid and my mother called the rematch with Grafton the most thrilling game they had been involved in, and it's my guess that most people who saw the game would agree.

*Brian Borland*

Glenda unstoppable under the basket.

The athletic Carolyn Nicholson warming up.

## CHAPTER 12
## IN THE PRESSURE COOKER

The Blue Devils and the Grafton team were giving a crowd of more than 13,000 heart failure. The game would not be decided until the final seconds.

Maynard got off to a hot start, leading 16-7. But after the first six and a half minutes, as my mom remembers, "We went dead."

Grafton came to life, and at the end of the first quarter only trailed 18-15. Grafton kept up its momentum through the second quarter, as Ruth Ann Buechele and Rose Marie Walke hit several shots. Walke, the girl who had shredded the Blue Devils in their first meeting, was starting to do it again as she tossed in two more buckets before the half to pace Grafton to a 34-29 intermission lead. The Blue Devils had been outscored 27-13 after their hot start.

Buechele and Walke started the second half even hotter and extended the Grafton lead. Maynard was down by 9 points early in the third quarter. The Maynard team needed a spark, and they got one from freshman Virginia Henniges. With most of the defensive focus on Carolyn and Glenda, Virginia, who only scored 8 points in the entire game, hit a shot with 6:29 left in the third quarter. That seemed to ignite the Maynard team. Carolyn and Glenda hit several tough shots to narrow the gap, and the third quarter ended with Grafton leading 47-43.

From the start of the fourth quarter to the epic ending, the game was a dogfight. Neither team ever held more than a 4 point lead. Late in the fourth quarter Maynard still trailed Grafton 51-47. Carolyn recalls this game as low scoring, with both teams playing a physical, scrappy game.

As Maynard trailed 53-50 with 2:23 left, Henniges, the lanky, improved freshman, who some said earlier was just the sixth girl on the squad, dropped in a 10 foot running jumper to pull Maynard to within 1.

Maynard guard Dorothy Fettkether snared the rebound after a Grafton miss, giving Maynard the ball down 1 point. Quickly getting the ball to Carolyn, Maynard made its move with 1:09 left when Carolyn hit Glenda, who turned, faked, and dropped in one of her short shots. That gave Maynard its first lead since the first quarter, but it was just a 1 point lead.

Fate, however, was with Maynard when Grafton star Ruth Buechele missed with a minute to go. Again, Dorothy Fettkether cleared the boards. Coach Kupferschmid called time out with 58 seconds left. Twenty seconds later, as Maynard tried to stall, Maxine Trettin fouled Glenda.

Glenda made her first free throw, putting Maynard up by 2, 55-53. But she missed the second, and while trying to get the rebound Henniges fouled Trettin. Buechele who was 16 of 21 from the free throw line was selected to shoot the free throws. Like Glenda, Buechele made her first attempt but missed her second, and the Maynard guards tied up the ball and forced a jump ball.

"Fettkether was the heroine as she controlled the tip to the freshman Barbara Fish," according to the Oelwein Daily Register's account of the game. Fish, as she had been coached to do, worked the ball to Carolyn Nicholson, and Maynard's ball control strategy was set in motion. Now, with 31 seconds to go clinging to a 55-54 lead, they started using stall tactics to try to run out the clock. Grafton needed to foul. Both Carolyn and Glenda remembered the Grafton coach running up and down the sidelines shouting, "Don't foul the Nicholsons! Don't foul the Nicholson girls!"

Carolyn and Glenda played keep-away until 9 seconds were left and they were forced to throw the ball to Virginia, the talented freshman. As soon as Virginia got the ball, she was fouled. Virginia went to the free throw line with Maynard up by 1 point and the game on the line. Carolyn and Glenda could see Virginia crying and shaking with tears running down her face as she was about to attempt the first free throw.

Carolyn, the senior star and team leader, remembers walking up to Virginia, giving her a big hug and saying, "It's no big deal, we are still up by 1 point. Whatever happens happens." Virginia calmly made both free throws.

And Maynard held on to win 57-54.

Newspapers reported that Grafton did not want to foul

the experienced Nicholson girls but wanted to foul the freshman in hopes that she would choke under pressure. "She Choked-Choked Grafton," the Oelwein Daily Register said.

I am sure Virginia Henniges got some comfort from her senior leader when she said, "We are still up one; it's no big deal." After the game, reporters asked Virginia about her free throws. The 14-year-old freshman said, "Oh my gosh, I was just afraid I was going to make them, I mean miss them." She was obviously still nervous when she answered the question. [15]

Virginia Henniges recently told me she had no idea how she kept her composure. Maynard shot only 43 percent against Grafton and scored 29 points below its average. Glenda scored 28 points and Carolyn had 21. Virginia Henniges only scored 8, but as my mom told me, "We would not have won without her 8 points."

In 2006, fifty years later, both my mom and Aunt Glenda laughed about those final seconds and hearing the Grafton coach yelling to not foul the Nicholsons. They both looked back and smiled, thinking that they both weren't sure they would have made both free throws.

Coming up next was the final act, the championship game. It would be against Garrison, a team Maynard had beaten three times during the season, by 12, 19, and 17 points. Did that mean the championship was in the bag for Maynard? Hardly. Other than the losses to Maynard, Garrison had lost only one game all season. And in those three losses, Garrison had learned an awful lot about Maynard's offense and its defense, an advantage some of the other teams that Maynard had played in the tournament had not had. And Garrison had a brilliant all-state player in high-scoring Sylvia Froning. Garrison would be no pushover.

After the Grafton game, Carolyn Nicholson was asked if the team was confident going into the final game. What she said, according to the Oelwein Daily Register, was "We want that game more than any we've ever played."

---

15 Oelwein Daily Register: John Meyer

*Spot Light on the Queens*

**Introduction Before Final Game with Garrison**

Photo courtesy of IGHSAU

CAROLYN NICHOLSON tried for two points in this semi-final action
as Maynard derailed the Grafton express 57-54 to revenge the only
defeat of the season. (Register Photo.)

2—Oelwein (Ia.) Daily Register        Saturday, March 3, 1956.

| GRAFTON | G | F | P |
|---|---|---|---|
| Buechele, f. | 7 | 16 | 2 |
| Seegers, f. | 4 | 5 | 1 |
| Walk, f. | 5 | 1 | 1 |
| Miller, g. | 0 | 0 | 2 |
| J. Wahl, g. | 0 | 0 | 0 |
| Trettin, g. | 0 | 0 | 4 |
| Totals | 16 | 22 | 9 |
| MAYNARD | G | F | P |
| C. Nicholson, f. | 7 | 7 | 3 |
| Henniges, f. | 3 | 2 | 0 |
| G. Nicholson, f-g. | 12 | 4 | 3 |
| Becker, g. | 0 | 0 | 4 |
| Fettkether, f. | 0 | 0 | 2 |
| Fish, g. | 0 | 0 | 3 |
| Roquet, g. | 0 | 0 | 0 |
| Totals | 22 | 13 | 15 |

Grafton .....15  19  13   7—54
Maynard ....18  11  14  14—57

Photo courtesy of the
Oelwein Daily Register

## CHAPTER 13
## THE BIGGEST GAME OF ALL

Of the 700 girls' basketball teams in Iowa, from big schools and small, only two were left standing in the State Tournament — Garrison and Maynard.

By Saturday, the day of the championship game, the Maynard girls had become celebrities. Western Union was raking in a bundle of money, as hundreds of telegrams had been sent to the girls at their hotel. And with all of the bouquets that were sent to the girls, they could have opened a flower shop.

Because the girls had been sequestered in the hotel since Tuesday and had been let out only for practice or games, they hadn't seen their friends or family members for the better part of a week. Carolyn was getting homesick and went to Coach Kupferschmid to arrange a special meeting to see her mom and dad before the big game. All that she wanted was a hug from her mom and dad. She got her wish. Carolyn was able to see Glenn and Ruth in the lobby Saturday afternoon for a brief moment, enough time to hug them.

The Maynard girls had never played four games in four days. They were tired and nervous, and they all were wondering how they would hold up in the championship game.

As Carolyn walked through the Kirkwood lobby heading off to the auditorium for the game, she spotted the front page of a newspaper. She remembered the headline reading, in big bold print, "Maynard the favorite, Carolyn needs 21." She was stunned, and she wondered what this was all about. Why did it say that Carolyn needed 21? Twenty-one what? She was upset.

All the media, coaches, teammates, and fans so desperately wanted Carolyn to score 1,000 points during her senior year. Glenda had already scored more than 1,000 points for the season, but Carolyn was 21 points short. She always said she couldn't care less about her point total. All she ever wanted was to win the state championship.

The media were so interested in the 21 points because never had two girls from the same Iowa team ever scored 1,000 each in the same season let alone two sisters. It was a huge deal to everyone but Carolyn.

By game time, 15,000 frenzied fans had packed Veterans Auditorium.

Maynard was confident going into the game because of its three victories over Garrison earlier in the season. Coach Koop was concerned that the girls might have been a little overconfident, in fact. He stressed that the previous three games against Garrison were in the past, and that the team needed to focus on the task at hand. Garrison was sure to have studied Maynard and would certainly be ready for the Blue Devilettes.

Ben Corbett, the coach of Garrison, and Mel Kupfer-schmid were good friends and had lots of respect for each other. In fact Corbett had been noticed in the stands cheering for Maynard in its battle against Grafton. Corbett wanted one more shot at Maynard. He wanted the opportunity to beat what he had earlier called "potentially the best team I have ever seen," as reported by the Oelwein Daily Register.

John Meyer later quoted Coach Kupferschmid as saying, "The previous three games mean nothing; I think this game is a 50/50 proposition."

Garrison had cooked up a surprise, a new and creative strategy, and they sprang it on Maynard right from the start of the game. Garrison knew that Carolyn was masterful at the pump fake and drive. Even with only two dribbles, Carolyn was so quick she could start from the top of the key, dribble twice and lay it in. The Garrison strategy for the first quarter was to have all three defenders surround Glenda. Carolyn couldn't drive and shoot and couldn't play her normal game because all the defenders were clogging the lane and the rest of the area around the basket. This frustrated Maynard. The strategy worked, and Maynard was behind 16-14 at the end of the first quarter.

During the time out at the end of the first quarter, Coach Kupferschmid sat Carolyn down and gave her unequivocal instructions: "Carolyn, you need to shoot. You have to shoot from the outside. Your pump fake and drive will not work while they are surrounding Glenda." By surrounding Glenda, Garrison was at the same time jamming the lane and blocking Carolyn's

Maynard 8 Miles 117

usual route to the basket. The notion of shooting from outside was foreign to Carolyn, since she scored most of her points driving to the basket. As the second quarter started, Carolyn heeded her coach's instructions and started shooting from outside. She made six outside shots in a row and scored all 12 of the Maynard points in the second quarter. She single-handedly outscored Garrison 12-8 in the second quarter, and Maynard led at halftime 26-24.

Throughout the first half, Garrison star Sylvia Froning kept her team in the game, living up to her all-state status. She scored almost 60 percent of her team's points for the game, with only two other girls on the team scoring any points. She did most of her damage in the first half, as the Maynard guards found ways to slow her down in the second half. Froning's torrid first half also provided a spark for Carolyn, whose competitive streak wouldn't allow her to be shown up by her archrival and fellow all-stater.

At the start of the second half, with Maynard leading 26-24 despite shooting well below their average, Garrison changed its strategy and started guarding Carolyn outside. Once that happened, Carolyn could use her patented pump fake and drive. It also opened up the game for Glenda, as now she only had one defender on her. Even though Garrison's Sylvia Froning poured in 33 points, Maynard would never relinquish its lead, and pulled away late in the game. The Waterloo Courier's headline read "Maynard Wins '56 Girls' Crown 62-51." Jack Ogden reported in the Des Moines Register:

"Powerful Maynard lived up to its championship tag, breaking loose in the second half here Saturday night to win the Iowa Girls' State Basketball title

Carolyn Nicholson, Maynard's all-state forward, turned in her finest performance of the tourney as she broke up Garrison's zone defense with dazzling drive-ins and deadly jump shots."

Maynard won the game, 62-51 and finished with a 32-1 record, thus fulfilling the prophecy that Glenda and Carolyn had carved into their bedroom wall as 8 and 9 year old girls. They had won the 1956 Iowa Girls State Basketball Tournament. I asked my mom how she felt going back to her bedroom for the first time as State Champs looking at the carved up wall. She paused and reflected, her mind racing back 50 years and said "Brian, our dreams came true."

My mom on the right holding the championship trophy.

Nearly 15,000 people jammed the huge Veterans Auditorium in Des Moines for the final game, here in progess.  Over 78,000 people attended the tournament.

Photo courtesy of IGHSAU

Carolyn Nicholson, Maynard's great out-forward, with hair flying, heads for tiny opening between Garrison's Delores Selk (44) and Jeannine Hagen (15). Glenda Nicholson is behind Selk.

Photo courtesy of IGHSAU

# Maynard Sets On Scoring Mark

Maynard became the first school in the history of girls' basketball to have two girls top the 1,000 point mark for a single season when Carolyn Nicholson hit 25 points.

That total gave her a season mark of 1,004 points. Her sister Glenda went over the 1,000 mark in the Blue Devils first tournament start against Albert City. She finished with 1,111.

The two were fourth and sixth in tournament scoring with Glenda netting 113 and Carolyn 101. Maynard's Virginnia Henniges was 13th in the tournament field with 48 points.

Carolyn moved to eleventh in the state all career scoring with 3,079 points — a record for out-forwards.

Courtesy of the Oelwein Daily Register

## Gem G: 'I DON'T CARE ABOUT SOME RECORD'

What of that newspaper headline Carolyn remembers seeing: "Carolyn needs 21"?

Toward the end of the championship game, fans, players and coaches were yelling at Carolyn to shoot. She didn't understand and didn't know why they were all yelling at her. She said she never thought about the record, even after seeing it mentioned hours earlier in the headline in the paper.

Then, with the game well in hand, Coach Kupferschmid called time out and said to the girls, "Carolyn needs only 4 points to get this record, and I want her to get it, so pass her the ball."

Carolyn was embarrassed and left the huddle, and for the first time she went against Coach Kupferschmid's wishes. She got Glenda and Virginia together and told them not to pass her the ball. "Let's just play this out," she said, "I don't care about some record. I just want to win the game."

As it turned out, Carolyn got fouled a couple of times and made a basket at the end of the game, finishing with 25 points. That gave her 1,004 points for the season and 3,079 for her storied career, and she and Glenda became the only two Iowa girls on the same team to score more than 1,000 points each in a season.

The new champs pose with their new trophy and the little blue dog, their good luck charm.

Coach Kupferschmid accepting the 1956 championship trophy.

## Bouquet Salute to Iowa's Cage Queens

Maynard's Nicholson sisters, Glenda (left) and Carolyn, find being girls' state basketball champions is really a bed of roses Sunday. Carolyn scored 25 points and Glenda 23 in Saturday night's 62-51 championship victory over Garrison. Carolyn finished her career with 3,079 points, eleventh best all-time mark.

Photo courtesy of the Oelwein Daily Register

## CHAPTER 14
## FROM ICE MAIDENS TO DANCING QUEENS

Coach Kupferschmid and the media had labeled the Maynard team as the most businesslike basketball team ever, and at their moment of supreme victory the Maynard players certainly lived up to that billing.

Although the Maynard Blue Devils had just become the Iowa girls' state champions, the players did not burst into a big celebration on the floor. There was no screaming and yelling, no tears of joy, no jumping up and down. The girls treated it the same as any other game - one they expected to win. In fact, all the attention made the girls a little uncomfortable, as it took a while for the magnitude of their achievement to set in.

I asked Carolyn and Glenda how they felt moments after the game. They agreed that both had a feeling that something was missing. They asked themselves "is this all there is for winning the state championship?"

They would soon find out what a big deal it was, when they learned what was happening in northeastern Iowa. At the time, that part of the state was not necessarily respected for its basketball talent, and the locals felt slighted. They responded enthusiastically when the Maynard team earned the respect they felt the northeastern part of the state deserved.

As the all-tournament team was announced on the floor after the game, five girls were called to center court to collect their all-tournament team awards. Carolyn's name was not called, so she assumed she didn't make it. Even though Carolyn always was supremely humble, she was a little surprised to think that she hadn't made the all-tournament team because she felt she had a pretty solid tournament. Then, Carolyn recalled the PA announcer proclaiming that "The last member and captain of the all-tournament team and the only unanimous choice for the 1956 State Tournament is Carolyn Nicholson." In those days the captain of the all-tournament team was the tournament's Most Valuable Player.

It took a moment, but suddenly it dawned on Carolyn that the player they were talking about was her. "Oh, that's me," she thought.

Press accounts of the game said glowing things, such as, "It was Carolyn Nicholson who kept Maynard in the game in the second quarter as she scored all 12 of her team's points with terrific outshooting," said Chuck Burdick of the Waterloo Courier. Other reporters commented that Carolyn, with her short stature and lightning feet, was the heroine of the tournament.

As the girls headed back to their hotel, they began to understand what they had accomplished. Once back in their hotel they started celebrating.

Coach Kupferschmid, who felt that it was important for the girls to do some celebrating, knew that Carolyn and Snooky were good jitterbug dancers who had won dance contests at school, so he asked them to dance in the lobby. Snooky recalled that Kupferschmid "had told us how other state champions had rolled all over the arena floor they were so excited." So at 3:00 a.m. the whole team joined Carolyn and Snooky in the lobby and rolled around on the floor, yelled, hugged, and cried. Snooky and Carolyn put on a jitterbug display for curious onlookers. For the first time in years, the Maynard team could truly celebrate.

Most of the girls got only about two hours of sleep that night.

After attending church the next morning, the Queens, as they now were being called, were treated to a spectacular breakfast. Then, six days after they had arrived in Des Moines, it was time to climb into the same three cars they had arrived in and head back to Maynard.

As they started the typical two and a half hour journey back home, they couldn't help but notice hundreds of fans in the streets of Des Moines, as trucks, cars, and buses joined their caravan on the way back to Maynard. Some idea of how popular they had become was beginning to sink in.

The caravan had to make an emergency stop as Irene Harrington's car had a flat tire. Several of the handy farm girls helped the local service station attendant fix the tire. The caravan was now in Marshalltown heading towards Maynard. Snooky remembers that hundreds of cars joined the caravan and all converged at the intersection of Highways 3 and 63, and the line had swelled to about 500 cars. By the time they pulled into Maynard, an estimated 5,000 people were waiting for them, waiting in a town whose whole population was 455. Nearby Westgate and Oelwein were already making plans to have their own separate celebrations for the Maynard Queens.

The team was scheduled to have a welcome home ceremony in the Maynard gym. But the crowd of well-wishers from all over Northeastern Iowa was too big for the gym, so they moved the ceremony to the baseball field.

After an hour of celebration at the ball field, the scene shifted to the jam-packed gym, where people had been waiting for hours. By then the cars were lined up on Maynard's main street for five miles, more than half way to Oelwein.

The Oelwein Daily Register covered the celebration as it moved to Maynard's tiny gym. Several speakers were on hand.

Mayor Earl Foss told the girls: "We had confidence in you. Everybody knows where Maynard is on the map. You put it there for the whole state to see."

Five members of the 1924 Maynard State Tournament team were on hand. One told the 1956 Blue Devils, "You did what we started out to do 32 years ago."

Team Captain Carolyn Nicholson spoke for all the Blue Devil traveling party when she said, "I'm glad that we could repay you fans for being so wonderful to us."

School Superintendent William Tock nicknamed Virginia Henniges "Icy" because she made those two clutch free throws in the semi-finals against Grafton.

Coach Kupferschmid ended his speech by introducing Carolyn Nicholson and calling her "The best girls' basketball player in the state."

The next day some sports writers credited Carolyn Nicholson for revolutionizing girls' 6 on 6 basketball. Up until that point most of the top scorers were tall, played under the basket, and were called post forwards. Carolyn, whose extreme quickness allowed her to use her pump fake and drive to the basket and who had also developed into a solid outside shooter, was now the all-time scoring leader from the out-forward position with a career total of 3,079 points. She had proved that an out-forward can be a great scorer. Experts credited Carolyn with helping create an entirely new offensive style.

The headline from the Des Moines Register read, "Typifies New Offensive Style." Brad Wilson wrote in part..."Carolyn's performance ranks alongside those of such outstanding girls as Garnavillo's Sandra Fiete." "The day of the one-girl offense is fast fading from the girl's scene." "Hard driving out-forwards and post-forwards who can shift in and out with ease was noticeable in offenses appearing in the 1956 finals."

Kupferschmid also credited Carolyn for changing the game, and he also says that Carolyn was more valuable to the team as the top assist player, team leader and quarterback.

At the end of the season, Kupferschmid wrote an article for the 1956 Iowa's Girls Basketball Yearbook. It brings tears to my eyes as my mom never talked about any of her accomplishments.

### Coach Proclaims Carolyn Nicholson, Maynard, the Greatest of Out-forwards

Carolyn drives around Barbara Beyer of Garrison to score one of her famous layups. Referee Sears of Creston makes ready to signal "it's through."

Photo courtesy of IGHSAU

## COACH PROCLAIMS CAROLYN NICHOLSON, MAYNARD, THE GREATEST OF OUT-FORWARDS:
### BY: COACH MEL KUPFERSCHMID

Carolyn Nicholson, 5 foot 4 inch, blue eyed, blond forward amassed many records while playing for Maynard. She is the leading scorer among outforwards in the history of the girl's basketball in Iowa. Carolyn tallied 3,079 points in her career. She also was an I.D.P.A. All-State selection for the past three years, and was picked by Des Moines Register this year.

Carolyn's scoring, outstanding as it was, was only a small part of her value to the team. She constantly passed up good shots in order to feed teammates for setups. Her first thoughts were always those of team welfare.

When practices would begin, Carolyn always was the first girl on the floor. She was a diligent trainer and established an excellent example after which the younger players could pattern themselves.

Carolyn did wonders in helping develop younger girls. She encouraged them if they had a particularly bad practice session.

Carolyn exhibited excellent poise and composure before and during important games. If Maynard needed a basket, I was always glad to see her get the ball, as she nearly always seemed to find a way to score, even when the odds seemed insurmountable. Carolyn was truly at her best when the odds were greatest.

### COMBINED ABILITIES

Other girls have been able to shoot more accurately than Carolyn. Many have rebounded better. Some have been better passers and defensive forwards, but I have never seen a girl combine the various talents so well. Along with these abilities there was a burning desire to excel.

Carolyn must have been something out of the ordinary to score so well despite her lack of height. As you look through the records of other outstanding scorers, they have nearly always been aided by exceptional height.

DILIGENT, POPULAR IN SCHOOL; A GOOD FARMER

Carolyn's abilities are not limited to basketball. She does her school work with the same diligence. At home she is quite an asset on her father's farm. She is extremely popular among the student body at Maynard.

When practices start at Maynard next fall, we will deeply miss all three of our graduating seniors, but especially we will miss the leadership and the general feeling of security and well-being that was present when Carolyn was on the floor. [16]

Photo courtesy of the Oelwein Daily Register

16 Iowa Girls High School Athletic Union: 1956 Yearbook 11th Edition Page 125

## Gem H: JUST WHO WAS THAT CUTE BOY?

Although the Maynard players didn't celebrate their victory as the game ended, several hundred Maynard fans rushed the floor.

An 18-year-old fan from Westgate named Carl Heller was one of those fans. Carl ran up to Snooky, picked her up and gave her a big hug. Snooky remembers, "I had no idea who this cute boy was, and he was lifting me in the air."

Carl introduced himself and boldly said, "I will be calling you." Carl did call. They started dating, and three years later they were married and enjoyed a wonderful life together.

NORTHEAST IOWA TURNED OUT enmasse to greet the Maynard Blue Devils home after the girls had won the state basketball championship in Des Moines with a 62-51 victory over Garrison. Cars and crowds jammed the Fayette county town for hours before the Queens arrived and steadily increased during the celebration which followed their return. (Register Photo.)

Photo courtesy of the Oelwein Daily Register

■ High School Girls' Basketball

*La Cañada's Sarah Borland scored a team-high 13 points to help the Spartans down Monrovia, 65-25, last Friday.*

Photo courtesy of Eric Danielson:The Outlook

The youngest great granddaughter of Glenn and Ruth Nicholson, Brooke Borland.
Photo courtesy of Mark Pajari

HARD TO TAKE: Sisters Kelly, left, and Kim Burns of Council Bluffs St. Albert console each other near the end of their loss to North Cedar.

Photo courtesy of Jeff Bundy: The World Herald

## Gem I: THE BASKETBALL GENE

Glenn and Ruth Nicholson had five children, who gave them 15 grandchildren and dozens of great grandchildren and some great-great grandchildren. They also produced very talented basketball players.

Their oldest daughter, Lou Ann, had Glenn and Ruth's first granddaughter named Kathy. Kathy's two girls, Kelly and Kim Burns, the great granddaughters of Glenn and Ruth, went on to lead St. Albert's Council Bluffs to the Iowa state finals in 2000. They were 27-0 going to the finals and lost a close final game.

Another great granddaughter of Glenn and Ruth's is Sarah Borland, the daughter of Glenn and Carolyn's oldest child, Brad. Sarah started as a freshman for her high school team in California and is a standout basketball player.

The youngest great granddaughter of Glenn and Ruth Nicholson is my daughter, Brooke. Brooke seems to have the basketball gene even at a very young age. She is left handed. She does everything else right handed except dribble a basketball. Of course Grandpa Glenn Borland claims she takes after him and his left hand.

The basketball gene pool that began in 1932 at the Buchanan County Fair seems poised to continue for generations and generations to come.

My mom was so proud of her younger sister, she was Glenda's biggest fan during the 1957 tournament.

## CHAPTER 15
## WHAT BECAME OF THEM?

### The 1956-'57 Team

Even without Carolyn, Snooky, and Dorothy Fish, who had graduated, and Dorothy Fettkether, who had left school, Maynard had another great season in 1956-'57.

Glenda, playing for the first time without her sister Carolyn, led Maynard to another state championship game. Garrison avenged its loss the year before to Maynard, winning a tense game 47-46. Glenda had scored 38 of Maynard's 46 points. In fact Glenda scored 61 points in the semi-final game to get Maynard to the title game.

Like Carolyn the year before, Glenda was named captain of the all-tournament team.

My mom, of course, had attended the final game and was absolutely crushed for Glenda when Maynard lost. The press followed Carolyn while she was in Des Moines. The headline in the Waterloo Courier read: "Carolyn greets Glenda" and the story went on to say: "Maynard's Glenda Nicholson, who topped all 1957 girls' state prep basketball tournament scorers, is greeted by her sister Carolyn, standing during the celebration at Maynard Sunday. Both were members of the Maynard state championship team last year, and both gained all-state honors. Carolyn is working in Oelwein."

### The 1957-'58 Team

In 1957-58 the school boundaries changed, and Randalia and Westgate joined the Maynard School District, thus the "West Central" designation. Mary Ann pointed out to me that only one girl from outside of Maynard made the team during their run and that was Darlene Dilly from Randalia.

The 1957-58 season would also be the first time since girls' basketball was resurrected at Maynard that the team would have no Nicholsons. On the heels of back to back appearances in the state championship game, and with a team that had evolved from a young group to a seasoned corps of juniors and seniors with tons of tournament experience and a coach who by now was a legend, Maynard was set for another run.

Led by Virginia Henniges and Mary Ann Roquet, Maynard tore through the regular season with a perfect 24-0 record, then won four tournament games, including the championship game to finish 28-0. In the championship game, Maynard beat Emerson 59-51.

**The 1958-'59 Team**

With Mary Ann Roquet, an all-state guard, the only player not returning, the 1958-'59 team looked even more promising. It got to the school's fourth consecutive championship game. Virginia Henniges was a senior now and playing in her fourth championship game, making her the only girl in Iowa history to play in sixteen State Tournament games. The championship game was against Gladbrook, and Maynard had beaten that team twice during the regular season. But Gladbrook beat Maynard in the final game, 72-60.

In an interview with me recently, Barb Fish made an interesting observation. She said that "Unlike the first three years, when we were in the state finals, in 1959 the fans actually started to cheer against Maynard, as this was our fourth straight year in the finals." She told me that unlike 1956 when 90% of the fans were cheering for Maynard, in 1959 "they cheered against us."

That's what happens when teams become dynasties. Any member of the New York Yankees of the 1950s or the UCLA men's basketball team of the 1960s and early '70s could attest to that.

The record books show Maynard as state champs in 1956, Maynard runner up in 1957, Maynard/West Central state champs 1958 and Maynard/West Central runner up 1959.

## CAROLYN NICHOLSON'S RECORD

Carolyn Nicholson turned down a partial scholarship offer to play at Iowa Wesleyan. Snooky recently told me, "I never understood why your mom didn't play in college. She was obviously good enough."

Coach Kupferschmid said Carolyn would have been a "magnificent college player." Regarding her decision not to accept the partial scholarship, he said, "I think romance might have had something to do with that." And, of course, he was right.

Carolyn's career scoring record for an Iowa out-forward, 3,079 points, held up for 13 years. In the late 1960s, 5'11" Denise Long, of Union-Whitten High, broke her record with an astonishing 6,250 total points. E. Wayne Cooley called Denise Long one of the greatest 6 on 6 players ever to play. Denise was so good that in 1969, the San Francisco Warriors of the NBA drafted her with their thirteenth pick. She was the first female ever drafted by an NBA team, though she never did play in the league. It got so much national attention that she was invited to appear on the Tonight Show.

Then, in 1987, 6'2" Lynne Lorenzen, of Ventura High School, surpassed Denise Long's record by totaling 6,736 points in her career. Her accomplishment was covered nationally by ESPN, USA Today and others.

## LOU ANN NICHOLSON

Lou Ann moved to and still lives in the Kansas City area and married a man named Rollis Kappmeyer. They have three children: Kathy, Kevin, and Kent.

## BETTY NICHOLSON

Betty stayed in Maynard and played basketball after high school for Brammer Manufacturing in a semi pro industrial league. She would marry Nathan Bly and have four sons: Steve, Scott, Richard, and Robert. Betty would give birth to twins Rick and Rob on the same day Carolyn gave birth to me, giving Ruth and

Glenn three new grandsons on June 26, 1963. Betty became vice president of Maynard Savings Bank and passed away September 25, 2013.

### GLENDA NICHOLSON

The 5'11" Glenda Nicholson accepted a partial scholarship to play 6 on 6 college basketball at Iowa Wesleyan. Her parents would have to pay some of Glenda's college costs. Surprisingly, Glenda, who had been a phenomenal scorer in high school, was recruited to play defense. And she proved to be a magnificent defensive player. She teamed up with Sandy Fiete, Maynard's old rival from Garnavillo. Glenda was a two time all-American and won a gold medal in the Pan Am Games in Chicago.

After her playing days were over, Glenda went on to be a very successful girls' basketball coach. Carolyn was so proud of her younger sister's success, she always wondered how much success she would have had herself at the college level.

Glenda married Eugene Thielbert and had two children, Lori and Mitch. She currently lives in Muscatine, Iowa.

Glenda, now in her mid-70s, told me this story: In a restaurant recently, a man approached Glenda and said to her, "Hey you are tall, did you ever play basketball?"

Glenda smiled and said "A little bit", and walked away.

### JIM NICHOLSON

The youngest of the Maynard children married Janice Gustin. They would have three children: Sheri, Ryan and Justin. The only Nicholson boy would buy the family farm from his dad and continue the Nicholson farming tradition until he sold the farm in the mid 1980's. Jim currently lives in a nursing home in Oelwein.

### FISH GIRLS

Marjorie Fish taught school in Cedar Falls, Iowa, Dorothy Fish spent many years as a teacher's aide, and Barb Fish worked as a nurse at St. Luke's Hospital in Cedar Rapids.

## SNOOKY AND MARY ANN

Marlene Snooky Becker got a teaching degree at Upper Iowa and taught for years in Oelwein. Mary Ann Roquet worked for nineteen years in the Western Union dispatch office.

## VIRGINIA HENNIGES

Virginia Henniges was a first team all-state choice two years in a row and was elected to the Hall of Fame of Iowa girls' basketball.

Mike McBride, a student at Oelwein high who was on the school's basketball team, had been dating Glenda Nicholson until Glenda went off to college. Then Mike saw Virginia play in a Maynard game and called her two days later for a date. Five years later they would get married. That's three Oelwein area boys chasing and marrying three Maynard girls: Glenn and Carolyn, Carl and Snooky, Mike and Virginia. To this day, they jokingly disagree on who pursued whom. The Oelwein guys claim the Maynard girls chased them, the Maynard girls claim the Oelwein guys pursued them. Regardless three happy, successful marriages were the result.

Two years after graduating from Maynard High School, Virginia Henniges enrolled in the School of Nursing in Waterloo, Iowa, graduated, and went on to become a nurse. She never gave college basketball a thought, because college basketball was simply not a common route for young women at the time. Virginia was more concerned with starting a family than she was with athletics, just like most of her peers.

In 1967, as Mike McBride describes it, "We almost lost Ginny." Mike and Virginia Henniges were in a terrible car accident. Virginia suffered a punctured lung and was minutes away from dying. A doctor performed emergency surgery and saved her life.

The McBrides settled in Milwaukee. They would have two daughters.

In 1973 outside of Prairie du Chien, Wisconsin, a drunk driver smashed into a car that was carrying one of Virginia and Mike's daughters, both Virginia's and Mike's parents, and two other passengers. Mike McBride got a phone call, and the doctor told him to get to La Crosse right away, "All I will tell you is your daughter is fine." Once the young couple arrived in La Crosse they heard the horrible news. All four of their parents had died. As I listened to them discuss this forty years later, I could see the pain still in their faces. I had no idea what to say next. I just felt privileged to be meeting Mike and Virginia McBride and felt a closeness to both of them.

I still have in my mind what the very talented and classy Virginia said to me when I asked about my mom. After 50 plus years she said "She was a great mentor for me."

### MEL KUPFERSCHMID

I talked with the 83-year-old Mel Kupferschmid in April of 2011. I wasn't sure where I wanted to begin. But he was. The first thing he said to me was "Yes, we did name one of our daughters after your mom. We thought the world of Carolyn."

I asked him about what he remembers when he first took over the Maynard program in 1954-55.

He said, "I knew the very first day of practice that the Maynard team was good. I was fortunate to inherit a great team." He said it was difficult the first year because he replaced his good friend Bill Mehle. Mel was first hired as the principal. It was an easy decision to take over the girls' basketball program.

Mel previously worked at Mount Union High School where he coached both boys and girls.

One particular challenge he brought up and still remembered more than 50 years later was when superstar Jean Overbeck transferred from Garnavillo to Monona for her junior and senior year. Mel said "That made Monona very strong."

Mel was soon promoted to superintendent of the school district, but kept his coaching duties. Mel Kupferschmid's five year run in Maynard was unprecedented. Mel's last official year coaching Maynard was 1959.

One thing he was always proud of: In the same calendar year of 1958 when his girls' basketball team won the State Tournament, four months later he coached the 1958 girls' softball team to a state title. Two state championship teams in four months.

His record as coach of the Maynard girls for five years was an amazing 140-9. And in those five years, his teams won the state championship twice and were runners-up twice. Four of his players Carolyn and Glenda Nicholson, Virginia Henniges and Mary Ann Roquet were inducted into the Hall of Fame of Iowa girls' basketball.

Mel Kupferschmid left the Maynard School District in 1960 to become a stock broker. He felt it was time for a career change.

He had a very successful business career, got married and started a wonderful life with his wife, Grace Ann. They had four children, the youngest named Carolyn.

Mel retired as a stock broker in 1985. Columbus High School in Waterloo, Iowa convinced him to coach again that year. Coach Kupferschmid rediscovered his winning ways and in 1990, Mel led Columbus to the State Tournament.

As my conversation with the 83-year-old Mel, who was suffering from Alzheimer's, was coming to an end, he said he wanted to be remembered as a guy who really supported and pushed for women's athletics.

He also said he followed very closely the career of Glenn Borland, my dad. "Glenn was a legend in Iowa" he said, "We were all so proud of him." Mel Kupferschmid died on February 16, 2013, at the age of 84. I am sad I did not complete this book while he was still with us. I am so thankful I was able to meet Coach Kupferschmid and spend precious time with him. My mom and the other players greatly loved, respected and admired their Coach. Mel Kupferschmid meant the world to his players and will never be forgotten.

### LATER MAYNARD TEAMS

After Maynard's incredible five year run under Mel Kupferschmid which ended with the Blue Devils winning 140 games and losing just 9, he left the program with high expectations for any incoming coach.

In the fall of 1962 Gene Klinge, who would become a coaching legend in Iowa, would continue the Maynard/West Central tradition. Gene would coach Maynard/West Central for 41 years and win over 800 games. He would lead the Blue Devils to several more state tournaments. During those tournament runs he coached several outstanding players including Deb Kuhne, Gail Meyers, Mary Parsons, Anne McFadden and dozens of others. He also coached Maynard's all-time leading scorer, Glenda Poock. In 1993 when Iowa voted to change from 6 on 6 to 5 on 5 Coach Klinge quickly transitioned his teams to the new 5 on 5 game. West Central remained successful throughout his career.

According to Max McElwain who wrote a fantastic book titled "The Only Dance In Iowa: A History of Six-Player Girls' Basketball," there was some controversy surrounding Deb Kuhne and the Maynard team. Deb was a very talented basketball player. Her mother had been sick for six years and died days before Deb went to high school. She enrolled as a freshman in 1968 at Starmont High School. Their farm was 25 miles away from Starmont High School but was in the Starmont school district. Maynard was less than ten miles away, but her farm wasn't in the Maynard district.

Deb and her father decided to transfer to Maynard, as it was closer. Deb's dad had to sell his cows and pigs to pay for the out-of-district tuition. At Maynard, Deb would join Glenda Poock, Gail Meyers, and others to form a very good basketball team. This caused a major controversy in the area, and it would shift the balance of power to Maynard/West Central. This was such a high profile deal that E. Wayne Cooley drove to Maynard to get involved. Deb was ultimately allowed to play for Maynard/West Central.[17]

Max McElwain went to Grandma Ruth's house in June of 1997. He spent the afternoon with Grandma Ruth, Betty, Carolyn, and Glenda, interviewing them about their playing days at Maynard. The details of that interview are in his book. [18]Max recently told me: "That afternoon was a wonderful experience for me. It was a beautiful sunny day. Ruth served lemonade and we talked for two hours. It was one of my favorite parts in the book. I had a really good time spending the afternoon with your grandmother, your mom, and your aunts."

In 1972, Glenda Poock, Deb Kuhne, and Gail Meyers would lead Maynard/West Central back to the State Tournament. Glenda Poock would end up scoring 3,993 points and become Maynard's all-time leading scorer. She would attend William Penn College in Iowa where she would play basketball and become an all-American.

A plaque on the wall at Maynard High School displays the scoring records, including:

#1 Glenda Poock- 3,993 pts
#2 Virginia Henniges- 3,126 pts
#3 Carolyn Nicholson- 3,079 pts
#6 Glenda Nicholson- 2,833 pts
#9 Deb Kaune- 2,549 pts.

Glenda Poock would later join former Maynard players Carolyn Nicholson, Glenda Nicholson, Virginia Henniges, Mary Ann

17 McElwain, Max. "The Only Dance In Iowa. A History of Six-Player Girls Basketball": Page 59-63.

18 McElwain, Max. "The Only Dance In Iowa. A History of Six-Player Girls Basketball": Page 73-77.

Roquet, and Irene Silka as members in the Iowa Girls' Basketball Hall of Fame.

Although the later Maynard/West Central teams were successful they were never able to match the success of Mel's five year run. The two state championships in 1956 and 1958 would be the only state titles Maynard/West Central would win.

THE TOWN OF Maynard was jammed packed Sunday during the victory celebration when the Blue Devils returned home with the girls state basketball championship. Crowds of people and cars packed the main street. (Register Photo.)

Photo courtesy of the Oelwein Daily Register

5,000 people packed Maynard to be part of the celebration. Cars were lined up for miles and miles. Photo courtesy of The Waterloo Courier

The 1956 championship was truly special to the Maynard community. The balcony in the tiny gym was packed during the celebration.
Photo courtesy of the Oelwein Daily Register

THE STATE champion basketball trophy was brought home and the Queens were crowned during a victory celebration in Maynard for the champions. Here the starting sextet crowds around the big trophy, left to right, Dorothy Fish, Carolyn Nicholson, Dorothy Fettkether, Glenda Nicholson, Virginia Henniges and Marlene Becker. (Register Photo.)

Photo courtesy of the Oelwein Daily Register

# IOWA DAILY PRESS

*First Team*

F—CAROLYN NICHOLSON
Maynard

F—SYLVIA FRONING
Garrison

My mom, first team All-State with her rival Sylvia Froning.

We, the Maynard Girls Basketball Team, wish to extend our sincere thanks to you for your messages and gifts of encouragement and congratulations. We feel we were successful in winning the championship because of the support received from you fine people.

| | |
|---|---|
| Carolyn Nicholson | Marlene Becker |
| Glenda Nicholson | Dorothy Fish |
| Virginia Henniges | Dorothy Fettkether |
| | |
| Donna Turner | Lois Arthur |
| Barbara Fish | Mary Ann Roquet |
| Sandra Potratz | Janice Hoehne |

| | |
|---|---|
| Mel Kupferschmid, *Coach* | Jean Meyer, *Cheerleader* |
| Irene Harrington, *Chaperon* | Deanna Franklin, *Cheerleader* |
| Lois Ingels, *Manager* | Eleanor Holmes, *Cheerleader* |
| Ann Bachman, *Manager* | Janice Meyer, *Cheerleader* |

Wm. A. Tock, _____ *Supt.*

## Gem J : THE MAYNARD 22

During Maynard's four year State Tournament run, from 1955-'56-1958-'59, only twenty-two girls played on those four teams.

That is remarkable. These are the twenty-two:

Lois Arthur 1956, 1957
Marlene Becker 1956
Darlene Dilley 1958
Dorothy Fettkether 1956
Barbara Fish 1956, 1957, 1958, 1959
Dorothy Fish 1956
Janet Garnier 1958, 1959
Virginia Henniges 1956, 1957, 1958, 1959
Janice Hoehne 1956, 1957, 1958, 1959
Sharon Jipson 1958, 1959
LaVonne Klammer 1957, 1958, 1959
Carolyn Nicholson 1956
Glenda Nichsolson 1956, 1957
Jane Nus 1959
Mardelle Parkinson 1958, 1959
Velda Poock 1958, 1959
Sandy Potratz 1956, 1957, 1958, 1959
Mary Ann Roquet 1956, 1957, 1958
Karen Simpson 1957, 1958, 1959
Deanna Steffen 1957, 1958, 1959
Donna Turner 1956, 1957, 1958, 1959
Lois Woods 1957, 1958, 1959

Shortly after the celebrations ended, my mom found time to pose in front of the headlines in the paper.

Mom back home reading the press clippings and day dreaming about Glenn.

## Gem K: CAROLYN'S DECISION

Some of Carolyn's friends and her basketball coach figured that her romance with Glenn Borland was the reason she didn't go to college. That was a factor, but that was only part of a complicated set of reasons.

Iowa Wesleyan College offered Carolyn a partial scholarship to play 6 on 6 college basketball. Wesleyan was one of the few colleges that played 6 on 6. It was also the only school that made any kind of offer to Carolyn. If they had offered her a full scholarship, she might have accepted.

She also had some self-doubts. Despite her long list of basketball accomplishments in high school, she questioned whether at 5'4" she would be able to compete in college ball.

Then there was the homesickness to consider. At one point after high school Carolyn took a job at the YMCA in Waterloo. After two weeks, she was so homesick and missed her mother so much that she quit and rushed back to the family farm. A couple months later she would get a job in Oelwein and rent a place just blocks from Glenn's parents' house as she wanted to feel close to Glenn and his family. She would live in that rented space until they were married a year later.

Carolyn's decision not to go on to college wasn't unusual, even for girls who were athletic superstars, in those pre-Title IX days. Women's sports in college didn't amount to much back then.

For Borland it was one of the greatest days in an up-and-down Big Ten career. The blond lefty, who waived his chances to go to

**GLENN BORLAND**

*Oelwein boy sinks Iowa*

Iowa to migrate to Madison in 1954, dropped in 16 points, second only to roommate Bob Litzow with 22. Borland was also the game's leading rebounder with 10. No Hawkeye snared more than seven.

The newly married couple say their goodbyes and head to Madison, Wisconsin.

## CHAPTER 16
## A GOOD YEAR AND A BIG DAY

By his junior year at Wisconsin, Glenn Borland had come a long way from being listed as the ninth-best forward on the freshman team. He was a starting forward, and his teammates elected him team captain.

Some newspaper headlines from that 1956-1957 season read, "Borland Leading UW Point Maker," (Associated Press) and "Can't Stop Borland's Hook." (Wisconsin State Journal).

When he played against Iowa his junior year, back in his home state, the Oelwein Daily Register said, "Oelwein basketball fans get a chance to watch their favorite son, Glenn Borland, on their TV." Tickets for that game were hard to get; thousands of fans wanted to see their local basketball hero play college ball in person.

Glenn was extremely excited for the game, his first real chance to play in front of his family, friends and hometown fans. Even more special was the opportunity to perform for his parents and girlfriend. It was a surreal experience to play against the team for which he had rooted throughout his entire childhood. The fans were similarly conflicted, as during the game dozens of normally loyal Iowa fans were instead cheering for Glenn. The game was close right down to the end. In the final minutes, Glenn grabbed a rebound despite being sandwiched between two taller Iowa players, then proceeded to make a 5-foot jump shot to put Wisconsin ahead for good.

After the epic battle against the Hawkeyes, the headline from the Cedar Rapids Gazette read "Oelwein Boy Sinks Iowa," and the headline from the Oelwein Daily Register "Borland Basket Beats Iowa Club." Glenn, playing in front of his home state fans, made the winning basket to beat Iowa.

The Badgers had a challenging season in 1956-1957, finishing 5-17 overall and 3-11 in the Big Ten. Glenn was the second leading scorer as a junior. Even though they had a difficult year, the team was improving and became much more competitive towards the end of the season. With all five starters coming back the future looked bright as all the kids were Big

Ten tested and ready for their senior season.

The summer between his junior and senior year of college included one particularly big day for Glenn and Carolyn Nicholson. Carolyn's friend Snooky recently told me, "Brian, when your mom and dad met, it was love at first sight. I knew my best friend would marry Glenn Borland." She was right. Glenn had proposed, Carolyn had said yes, and the couple decided to get married on August 18, 1957, at the Zion Lutheran Church in Oelwein.

The engagement was big news in the Oelwein/Maynard area. The buzz was that two basketball stars were getting married. The headline in the Oelwein Daily Register said "Engaged to Glenn Borland," with a beautiful picture of Carolyn.

Several of Glenn's teammates and Madison friends would make the trip to Oelwein. Some teased Glenn, "Where the heck is Oelwein?" They had no idea how to get there. Included in that group was Glenn's teammate and good friend Steve Radke. He was in the wedding party as a groomsman. Steve recently recalled the special day and remembered getting lost several times on the way to Oelwein.

Hundreds of close relatives and friends attended the wedding. I recently talked to my dad about their special day. He was so happy that so many of his Badger teammates made the trip to Oelwein. He also remembers as humble as Carolyn was, she didn't want any media attention or any media attending the wedding, even though they had been following the story for months. My dad recalled, "It was a picture perfect day. We had all our family and close friends around us." Carolyn didn't want a fancy reception or dinner so they had the reception in the basement of Glenn's small house, with washtubs filled with refreshments. My dad remembers how close the Borlands and the Nicholsons became. He was very proud that Glenn and Linda and Glenn and Ruth became close friends. In the end all that my mom wanted was a simple wedding celebrating with her family and close friends. That is what she got. Later in the night a pickup basketball game did break out as the groomsmen found the 9 car garage and Glenn's childhood basketball court. No report on the winners, though it was doubtless a spirited contest.

Barb Fish recently told me that the marriage between Glenn Borland and Carolyn Nicholson was "The dream marriage."

An interesting article appeared in Oelwein Daily Register the next day:

Remember when we dreamed a breed of super basketball players?...You'll be glad to know Maynard's pretty Carolyn Nicholson, All-State, married Oelwein's handsome Glenn Borland, Captain elect of the Wisconsin Basketball Team. Sign up their kids!

Although their kids, myself, Brad, and Liz, didn't turn out to be supernatural basketball stars, we all were very good players and, I hope, even better human beings.

It was called the "dream" Marriage -August 18, 1957.

# Chamberlain's 32 Points Spearhead Comeback Victory

| Wisconsin—62 | fg | ft | pf | Kansas—83 | fg | ft | pf |
|---|---|---|---|---|---|---|---|
| Borland,f | 5 | 2 | 2 | L.Jhnson,f | 1 | 0 | 1 |
| DeMerit,f | 2 | 0 | 2 | Elstun,f | 7 | 1 | 4 |
| Litzow,f | 8 | 0 | 5 | Johnston,f | 4 | 3 | 2 |
| Gross,c | 2 | 1 | 5 | Green,f-c | 0 | 0 | 1 |
| Radke,c | 0 | 0 | 1 | Jett,f | 0 | 2 | 0 |
| Telfer,c | 0 | 0 | 2 | Chmbrln,c | 9 | 14 | 2 |
| Holt,g | 0 | 0 | 0 | Parker,g | 1 | 3 | 4 |
| Kulas,g | 6 | 9 | 3 | King,g | 6 | 2 | 5 |
| Lehtfuss,g | 1 | 0 | 0 | Hollinger,g | 0 | 0 | 1 |
| Rogneby,g | 0 | 2 | 5 | Kindred,g | 0 | 0 | 1 |
| | | | | Dater,g | 0 | 0 | 0 |
| | | | | Cleland,g | 1 | 0 | 0 |
| Totals | 24 | 14 | 25 | Totals | 29 | 25 | 21 |

Half: W 38, K 30.
FTM: W 16, K 15.

Courtesy of Wisconsin State Journal

Glenn Borland's left handed hook shot was unstoppable, even in college.
Photo courtesy of The Capital Times/Wisconsin State Journal

Can't Stop Borland's Hook

Glenn Borland of Wisconsin lets go with one of his patented left-hand hooks as Michigan's M. C. Burton misses an attempted block in Monday night's game. The Badgers won, 70-65.
—State Journal Photo by Arthur M. Vinje

Photo courtesy of the Wisconsin State Journal

## Gem L: GLENN vs. WILT CHAMBERLAIN

On Saturday, December 22, 1956, Glenn played against the best college basketball player in the nation, 7'1" Wilt Chamberlain, the star player for the Kansas Jayhawks, and one of the greatest basketball players of all time.

My dad's job as a 6'1" forward was to double team and steal the ball from Chamberlain. He would wait until Chamberlain put the ball on the floor and then try to steal it. Glenn had four steals during the game and frustrated Chamberlain. On the last attempt to steal the ball, he fell into Chamberlain's legs and dropped to the ground as a foul was called. As my dad was lying on the ground, Wilt simply grabbed the basketball in the palm of one hand and lifted Glenn off the floor with the other. My dad felt relieved that Chamberlain just "set" him down.

Kansas beat Wisconsin 83-62. The next day the Wisconsin State Journal reported on the game. The headline read "Chamberlain's 32 Points Spearhead Comeback Victory" In front of 10,000 fans the Badgers had a 38-30 halftime lead. The final score was 83-62. With 6 minutes to go Wisconsin actually lead 56-55, but Wisconsin would not score a basket the rest of the game and managed to make only six free throws as Chamberlain dominated on the defensive end not allowing another shot through the hoop. Though Wisconsin held Chamberlain to his third lowest point total of his young career he finished with 32 points. He made 14 straight free throws at the end of the game allowing Kansas to pull away. Playing against and guarding Wilt Chamberlain is another experience Glenn would never forget.

The article also stated that the Badger forwards provided a spark as Bob Litzow tallied 16 and Glenn Borland added 12.

# Borland, Holt Honored

## Voted Badger Cage Captain, Most Valuable

Glenn Borland, senior forward form Oelwein, Ia., Tuesday, was named captain of the 1957-58 University of Wisconsin basketball team, the second straight year his teammates voted him the honor.

Wisconsin also named the most valuable, voting that honor to Walter (Bunky) Holt, senior guard from Evansville, Ind.

Announcement of the two honor selections was made Tuesday night when the Madison Gyro club honored players and coaches at its 35th annual basketball banquet.

Among those taking part in Tuesday night's Gyro club Wisconsin basketball banquet was the quartet pictured above. Left to right are Harold E. (Bud) Foster, Badgers' head coach; Walter (Bunky) Holt, most valuable player; Glenn Borland, captain; and Fred (Fritz) Wegner, assistant coach.

—State Journal Photo

Photo courtesy of the Wisconsin State Journal

## Collegiate Career Ending

Among those winding up their collegiate basketball careers this weekend in Wisconsin's final two games is Glenn Borland, above, senior reserve forward from Oelwein, Ia. Borland, a regular last year, has seen little action in the current campaign, but came up Monday night to score 12 points against Minnesota. The Badgers, who play at Northwestern Saturday night and close at home against Michigan Monday, could finish in the Big 10 cellar for the first time since 1919.

Photo courtesy of The Capital Times/
Wisconsin State Journal

## CHAPTER 17
## LIKE A BAD DREAM

Glenn's senior season looked to be a special season for the Badgers. All five starters were coming back including Glenn and Bob Litzow, the top two scorers. Also returning were Walter Holt and Steve Radke. Before the season began, newspapers flashed headlines like "Litzow most valuable, Borland UW Captain" from the Wisconsin State Journal.

Glenn was again elected team captain. Things looked pretty good for Glenn. In the end, however, his final season would unfold like a bad dream and it would shape his character forever. Wisconsin had recruited several players whose high profile backgrounds stirred great expectations. Most of them had played on the Badger freshman team the previous year.

The college basketball air was heavy with politics in those days, and it was made clear during the recruiting process that whoever recruited certain players would need to make a commitment that they would play immediately, which in those days would be their sophomore season. If some of these players didn't play, UW would have a tough time successfully recruiting other players from those players' home regions. This situation put Coach Bud Foster in a tough position. Bud, who recruited Glenn and gave him his opportunity and a scholarship, now had to decide what to do with his senior team leader and captain.

With the 1957-58 season about to start, Coach Foster had to decide whether to play a team favorite, the team captain and one of the best players or to not play that person and adhere to the pressures of recruiting and outside influences.

Bud Foster chose not to play Glenn Borland. The very first practice of the 1957-58 season, Glenn's senior season, Glenn found himself on the second team along with his friend and teammate Steve Radke. Glenn, the second leading scorer from last year and Steve Radke, for some reason, had lost their starting positions during the off-season.

When the starting line-ups were publicly announced before the first game, the media people were shocked to find three sophomores and two seniors in the starting lineup.

With the expectations so high, the season turned into a major letdown, not just for Glenn and Steve, but the entire team.

Glenn saw very limited action, playing in only thirteen games and scoring only 35 points. Before one Big Ten game the papers reported three starters were hurt and would be unable to play. The headline from the Capitol Times read "Crippled Badgers Open Big 10 Race Saturday." Still Glenn never got into the game. Not starting Glenn might be understandable, but why wouldn't he be in the rotation as the first or second player off the bench?

Throughout the season Glenn and Steve were on the second team. And all season long that second team would beat the first team during practice.

At the start of every game, Glenn would be at center court shaking hands with the opponent's captains only to return to the bench to watch others play the game.

The Badgers, with Glenn on the bench, ended up last in the Big Ten. The headlines in the Capitol Times read "Michigan Trounces Wisconsin," "Badgers Finish in Last Place," and "Hit Bottom In Big Ten."

Glenn never complained, never got down on himself, not once.

I asked him how he could keep his cool and not get upset and not confront the coaches. He said "I just tried to keep my head up and continue to be the team leader and captain." I've often wondered what his new wife, herself a Hall of Fame basketball player, was thinking of the unlikely situation in which Glenn found himself.

At one point, Foster suggested that Glenn's height, 6'1 ½", was the reason he was relegated to the bench. But the player who took Glenn's place wasn't significantly taller than him. He was 6'4", just a couple inches taller than Glenn. The question of height does not explain why Foster didn't play Glenn at least as a key reserve.

I recently had a chance to meet four of Dad's teammates at an alumni game. I asked them to explain to me why he didn't play and what they remembered about that senior year in 1958.

They had been laughing and joking, but when I asked my question, they got serious and said things like:

"We needed Glenn, our team captain."

"We all wanted him to play and knew he should be playing."

"As young kids we didn't understand why one of our best players and team captain wasn't playing. Bud Foster has passed away, so we may never know the entire story."

All the players remember the speech Foster made at the end-of-the-season banquet. With tears in his eyes when it was Glenn's turn to collect the team captain award, Bud Foster said, "The biggest mistake I have made in my life was not playing Glenn Borland this season. I hope you can forgive me." The headline in the Wisconsin State Journal from the banquet read "Borland, Holt Honored."

We will never know the regrets that Bud Foster held inside or what really led him to sit Glenn Borland that season.

After the banquet, Foster, who was on the hot seat with the Badgers finishing in the Big Ten cellar, was summoned to a meeting of the UW athletic board. When asked by a reporter if the meeting would be about his future, Foster replied "Well, I don't think they asked me to come in to talk about the future of the fencing team," according to the Des Moines Register.

Bud Foster was fired. The following summer incoming coach John Erickson crossed paths with my dad, by then a UW graduate. Erickson stopped Glenn, introduced himself and said, "I've been watching film of your team over the past two years. Why in the world were you not playing?"

Glenn's response, "I have no idea."

Glenn acknowledges that the ordeal of his senior year had a tremendous impact on the rest of his life. He taught his own kids that life is not always fair. Take what you get, be nice, and respect everyone. These lessons would help him to go on to achieve an unbelievable career as a father, teacher, coach, and a school administrator impacting thousands of lives.

# Last of era leaves job as leader of schools

## Glenn Borland retires; friendly legacy remains

**By Debbie Stone**
Education reporter

Listening to Glenn Borland tell how the baker at Copps grocery made him a special batch of glazed doughnut holes last week, it's easy to understand why people like him so much.

"I got there and they only had blueberry and cherry ones. I don't go for those very much so I asked, 'Don't they make plain glazed doughnut holes anymore?' And the woman told me, 'We're all out right now, but I can make you some.' And then she did, right on the spot. Yep, she did."

And with a devilish smile that makes his 58-year-old face turn into a child's, he popped one of the morsels into his mouth. "Boy, these are good!"

You'd better believe Borland won't forget that baker. Every time he walks into her store, he'll mention that gesture. And he'll thank her again, and again, and again.

Small gestures mean as much to Borland as big ones.

And people with less prestigious jobs are as important to him as those with prestigious ones.

That's one of the reasons he's so beloved in the Madison School District, where he's worked up the ranks for 36 years to become coordinating superintendent, the second-in-command. He's the guy who runs the day-to-day operations of the 24,000-student system.

"This is somebody of real importance and he always took time for us little women in the kitchen," said Wanda Braund, chief food service worker at Whitehorse (formerly Schenk) Middle School. "He always said, 'Got any problems, Wanda, you let me know.' He's an excellent person."

Borland — known as "Borley" or "Glenny" to his friends and relatives — is retiring at the end of this month to spend more time with his wife of 37 years, Carolyn; his three children, Brad, 35; Brian, 31;, Liz, 29; and his 2-year-old granddaughter, Amanda.

State Journal photo/L. ROGER TURNER

Glenn Borland's approaching retirement as the second-in-command in Madison schools makes him remember his arrival in Madison to play basketball at UW-Madison. His first school district job was teaching physical education at West High in 1956.

His leaving marks an end of an era in the Madison schools.

He's one of the last of a group of men hired in the late 1950s, mostly former jocks, who climbed to the highest echelons of the district bureaucracy.

Borland's sport was basketball. A 6-foot-1-inch forward in college, he was captain of the UW-Madison men's basketball team during his junior and senior years, and was known for miles around as "the old lefthander," for his lefthanded hook shot.

"We were just . . . a kind of fraternity," said Sam Barosko, former principal of Sennett Middle School. "We were task-oriented, but we drank our beer together, too."

In 1956, Borland was hired as a physical education teacher at West High School. He moved from there to Memorial High School, where he became the head basketball coach.

In 1969, he was promoted to assistant principal at Memorial, and six years later,

Please see **BORLAND**, Page 3C

Photo courtesy of Wisconsin State Journal

## Gem M: GLENN THE EDUCATOR

After he graduated from the University of Wisconsin, Glenn Borland went on to have a rich and happy family life as well as a rewarding career as an educator and coach. His first job after college was as a physical education and history teacher at West High School in Madison. He also coached three sports at West. He interrupted that job for a six-month active duty stint as an Army lieutenant in a military police unit, after which he did several years of Army Reserve service.

His next job was as teacher, head basketball coach, and athletic director at James F. Madison Memorial High in Madison, where he went on to become assistant principal.

When Glenn was 36, he and the family moved to Austin, Minnesota, where Glenn was principal of Austin High School for three years. They returned to Madison in 1975 when Glenn was offered the job of principal at La Follette High School.
He was promoted to assistant superintendent for elementary education, then in 1992 he was named interim superintendent of Madison schools. He held that job for one year, and retired in 1994 after a permanent superintendent was hired.
Glenn was inducted into the Madison Sports Hall of Fame in 2008.

If my dad had gone into business, he would probably have been a rich man, maybe as CEO of a major company. He chose to stay in education because he loved to work with kids and wanted to make a difference. In his mind real wealth was having a good family life, spending time with close friends and helping others.

Glenn and Carolyn had three children: my brother Brad, my sister Liz, and me, and they had six grandchildren and hundreds and hundreds of friends. Brad Borland married Maureen Gupta and lives in California with his three children: Amanda, Sarah, and Tyler. Liz Borland has been a dedicated nurse for over twenty years and lives in Monroe, Wisconsin.

# Borland in a league of her own

The next morning, back in Maynard, the streets were lined with people. Every storefront had a banner in the window. The gym itself was packed. .

It was estimated that a crowd of 3,000 had shown up in the tiny town, with its population of 458, to honor the Maynard girls basketball team, which had just won the 1956 Iowa state high school championship.

But the night before, Carolyn Borland was insisting Wednesday, she hadn't realized what a big deal it was. She was Carolyn Nicholson then, and she and her sister, Glenda, had led Maynard to the title in front of a frenzied crowd in the Des Moines Veterans Auditorium.

Carolyn knew how hard they had worked and how far they had come, but with the final buzzer, and a 62-51 win for Maynard over Garrison, she had a small sense of, "Is this all there is?"

How could a high school senior have known that what it was really all about was memories?

Carolyn Borland has been thinking about these things lately, and not just because she was back in Maynard a couple of weeks ago to see the farmhouse where she grew up and started shooting baskets outside when she was four years old. In those days Maynard didn't have a girls team and Carolyn would listen to the state tournament on the radio and hope one day she might get a chance to play. By the eighth grade, she did.

Carolyn has been reliving that time because her son, Brian Borland — after accompanying his mom on a 2006 trip to Iowa commemorating the 50th anniversary of Maynard's state championship — has begun to write a book

Borland family photo

Carolyn Nicholson Borland during her high school basketball playing days in Maynard, Iowa.

spun from the "Hoosiers"-like victory of the tiny school that beat all comers in the highly competitive arena that was Iowa girls basketball.

It's a basketball story and a love story, too. Just a couple of years out of high school, Carolyn wed Glenn Borland, who grew up eight miles from Maynard in the town of Oelwein. Glenn was on a basketball scholarship at UW-Madison and Carolyn joined him here when they married. They're still together and still here, in a home on the West Side.

Glenn played well for the Badgers, competing against Wilt Chamberlain and Kansas and scoring the winning basket in a game against Iowa. "Iowa Boy Beats Iowa," one headline read. Glenn eventually became better known in this area as a high school coach, athletic director and administrator, and in

2008 he was inducted into the Madison Sports Hall of Fame. Gov. Jim Doyle, who played basketball for Glenn at Madison West, has offered to write a foreword for Brian's book.

Carolyn was inducted into the Iowa Basketball Hall of Fame in 1971. Highlights of her storied career included scoring 54 points in one game as a sophomore and hitting nearly 80 percent of her free throws in her senior year. That season she and Glenda became the first two teammates to each score more than 1,000 points.

In 2006, the family went to Des Moines for the girls state tournament, where the 1956 Maynard team was honored at halftime of the championship game. Earlier, at a breakfast, Carolyn sat next to the governor. Her kids, now grown, watched wide-eyed. Carolyn had

Brian Borland

Carolyn Nicholson Borland, during a 2006 trip to Iowa commemorating the 50th anniversary of the Maynard High School girls basketball team winning the Iowa state championship.

rarely mentioned her high school playing days. Brian recalled his Mom's old coach, Mel Kupferschmid, now living outside Seattle, saying Carolyn was "the straw that stirred the drink."

Certainly that was true in the 1956 title game against Garrison. Carolyn's taller sister, Glenda, had been Maynard's primary offensive weapon during their title drive. But in the championship game, Garrison unveiled a defense that collapsed several players around Glenda under the basket. There was no getting the ball to her.

In the second quarter, Kupferschmid, the coach, called Carolyn over and told her she had no choice but to shoot. Carolyn responded by hitting seven straight baskets from the perimeter, giving Maynard the halftime lead, and, eventually, the championship.

In the moments afterward, Carolyn recalled this week, they announced the all-tournament team on the public address. Four names were called and then the announcer proclaimed "the only unanimous choice and captain of the all-tournament team."

Carolyn said, "It was me."

Contact Doug Moe at 608-252-6446 or dmoe@madison.com.

On October 7, 2009, Doug Moe spent time with my mom and dad as they invited him into their home. The next day this article appeared in the Wisconsin State Journal. Doug would later tell me: "What a special morning it was for me spending time with your mom and dad".
Photo courtesy of Wisconsin State Journal

## CHAPTER 18
## THE END OF AN ERA: SUNDOWN FOR 6 ON 6

No person in the United States shall, on the basis of sex, be excluded from participation in, be denied the benefits of or be subjected to discrimination under any education program or activity receiving Federal financial assistance.

Sec 901(9) Title IX Education Act, 1972
(Better known as Title IX)

Title IX, which was intended to provide equality to female athletes, would ultimately spell the end of one of the most successful high school girls' sports programs in U.S. history, Iowa girls' 6 on 6 basketball.

Starting in 1972, E. Wayne Cooley had a major problem. Congress enacted Title IX into law, and the federal government was coming after him and the Iowa Girls High School Athletic Union. The government challenged the IGHSAU, claiming that 6 on 6 and the Union's unique rules were not legal.

The government maintained that the rules of 6 on 6 put Iowa girls who wanted to play 5 on 5 college basketball at a big disadvantage. The rationale for opposing 6 on 6 was that an Iowa girl who only played defense couldn't adapt and be effective playing both offense and defense in 5 on 5 in college.

Colleges all over the country were under pressure from Title IX to develop women's sports programs. If they didn't they would miss out on huge amounts of federal money. Basketball was an obvious choice for expansion, so colleges were adding women's basketball, and most chose to add 5 on 5. For the first time, high school girls were in demand to play college sports, and it was argued that schools would pass over 6 on 6 players when scholarships were handed out.

Advocates of 6 on 6 countered that nationally the Iowa girl was doing very well. In fact Jim Duncan in the Palimpsest wrote, "Coaches have developed the Iowa girl until it is truly national in scope. For three decades, more than one out of five first All-Americans have come from Iowa." During the 1940s,

50s and 60s roughly 20% of the All-Americans came from Iowa. [19] That's how good the 6 on 6 girls were. The supporters argued that if you were a good enough 6 on 6 player in high school you could successfully adapt to 5 on 5.

Thus the central question of the debate was: Which is more important, the tradition and popularity of 6 on 6, or the possibility of greater future scholarship opportunities for the girls by switching to 5 on 5?

That debate didn't exist during the heyday of Iowa girls' 6 on 6, the 1940s, 50s, and 60s, because most of the girls, in other states as well as in Iowa, didn't expect to play college basketball. One reason was that there were a lot fewer women's college teams than in the post Title IX years. Only the really good players tended to play in college.

The debate was heated, and it brought national media attention to Iowa. Several women's rights groups were fighting against 6 on 6. These groups wanted equality in all measures for men and women, and that meant the opportunity to play the same game. Unfortunately, they simply ignored the success of the 6-on-6 game in Iowa

During the 1983-84 season, three Iowa high school girls filed a lawsuit against the IGHSAU claiming 6 on 6 was not equal to 5 on 5, thus not compliant with Title IX. They claimed they were being discriminated against by not having the opportunity to play 5 on 5 in high school, thus not being prepared for college.

Even in the Iowa Legislature, Wayne Cooley, who had vigorously promoted and protected Iowa girls' basketball, was criticized by lawmakers for not including women on the Union's board and was accused of not being in touch with the female athlete.

Cooley, knowing that 6 on 6 was part of the lifeblood of rural Iowa, needed to react. And, of course, he did.

He came up with a solution during the 1984-85 season:

---

19 Duncan, Jim 1968. The Palimpsest,Vol. XLIX No. 4 Page 156 The State Historical Society of Iowa, April 1968

- The Iowa Union would offer both 5 on 5 and 6 on 6.
- There would be two separate girls' state tournaments, with two state champions.
- Each high school would be allowed to vote on which style it wanted to play.

As expected, 6 on 6 remained much more popular than 5 on 5.

As time went on, women's programs became more popular at the college level, leading more and more Iowa high schools to switch to 5 on 5. By 1993, the writing was on the wall, as coaches, players, parents, and even Cooley realized that the Iowa Girl needed to play 5 on 5 like the rest of the world.

So, sixty years after the 6 on 6 rules were established, the Iowa Girls High School Athletic Union did what had been the unthinkable: On February 3, 1993 the Union voted to end 6 on 6 girls' basketball. Maynard High, now called West Central, hung on to its 6 on 6 program until the very end. The community was proud of its history of success and was saddened when they were finally forced to switch to the 5 on 5 game.

E. Wayne Cooley supported the decision. His goal was always to promote and protect the Iowa Girl. Cooley, who ran the IGHSAU from 1954-2002, passed away on May 11, 2013, he was 90 years old. My mom always talked about Mr. Cooley and thought the world of him, as did the thousands of Iowa girls who had the honor of playing 6 on 6. He will be remembered as an icon in Iowa and the man who was credited for running one of the most successful girls' high school programs in the history of the United States.

When the decision was made to end 6 on 6, it went largely unnoticed by the rest of the country. By then, most of the country had no idea what 6 on 6 was.

But several generations of Iowa Girls who were part of the 6 on 6 phenomenon were heartbroken.

My Aunt Glenda's opinion, however, surprised me. She sympathized with the girls who only played defense in high school. "Brian," she said to me, "the girls were at a disadvantage if they never played offense before. As sad as it was, they needed to change the game." Glenda had a good perspective, because she was part of the small percentage of girls who had the ability to play in college.

Iowa 6 on 6 girls' basketball will always be remembered as the sport that gave an estimated one million Iowa girls a chance to play competitive sports. Girls' basketball helped give identity to hundreds of small Iowa towns. The lucky people who lived through the glory days of 6 on 6 will never forget or under-appreciate what the game meant to the state of Iowa. And the hopes and dreams of hundreds of rural communities will never be forgotten.

The popularity of Iowa girls' 6 on 6 basketball during that period will never again be equaled by any sport on that scale for either gender. The current Iowa girls' state tourna-ment, which is 5 on 5, is no match for what it was in the 6 on 6 days of yesteryear.

I have talked with dozens of women who played 6 on 6 basketball. They all have memories that will last a lifetime and will be passed down to future generations. I know I will never forget what I have learned about the experiences of my mother and her teammates.

As Barb Fish recently told me, "It is still one of the big-gest moments in our lives. Brian, 50 years later I still dream about it."

The Iowa girls 6 on 6 State Tournament was a magical event. The coaches, players and fans will never forget what girls basketball meant to the state of Iowa.  Photo courtesy of IGHSAU

In March 2006, 50 years after winning the state title, coach Mel Kupferschmid with Glenda and Carolyn.

As their names are called, Carolyn and Glenda Nicholson wave to the sold out crowd and walk off the court one last time together.

## Gem N: THE REUNION

One day in January of 2006, I was at my parents' house, and I overheard my mom and dad discussing an invitation they got in the mail. I asked what it was for. My mom casually said "Oh they want to honor our 1956 team during the 2006 State Tournament to celebrate the 50th anniversary of Maynard winning the State Tournament. Do you think you want to go?"

She had never told me about her remarkable basketball career, so I knew almost nothing about it. I didn't know the story of the 1956 Maynard team because in all of my 42 years she had never talked about it. I said, "Mom, of course I am going. It will be the highlight of the year for me."

That trip would end up changing my life. I would never look at my mom the same again.

During the weekend of the tournament/reunion, I acted as a reporter. At the hotel in Des Moines, I used a camcorder and interviewed my mom and Glenda, asking lots of questions about that 1956 team. I have about two hours of great footage as they shared their story about what happened fifty years before, and much of what they said is recounted in this book.

I was able to interview and document on video most of Mom's teammates. I also had the honor to meet and spend time with Coach Mel Kupferschmid.

Mom's 1956 Maynard team was introduced and honored during halftime of the girls' state championship game. I videotaped the ceremony from the center court as I broke through security and said I was taping all of this for a documentary (kind of true). Each player was introduced and their happy and proud faces were projected on the huge scoreboard as highlights from the 1956 championship game played in front of the sold out arena.

I had chills all over my body and tears in my eyes and was

shaking during the entire program. I learned that night that my mom was the unanimous pick for the 1st team All-State and at the time held the all-time scoring record for out-forwards. In 1956 she was the tournament captain and most valuable player of the State Tournament. Incredibly, all of that was news to me. I had never fully understood how gifted she was. I always knew she was a special person, but not as an athlete. Why didn't she ever talk about this? I played basketball my entire life and never recalled her talking about how good she was and how great their team was.

After watching the celebration I was stunned, proud, and honestly a bit mad all at the same time. I was 42 years old, I had not understood that my mom had been a high school superstar. Why didn't my parents ever talk about this? I made a promise to myself that night I would never forget this moment and the strong feelings I had. As I researched all this, I came to realize my mom, Carolyn Nicholson Borland, was one of the most humble people in the world.

Most of her current friends had no idea Carolyn had even played basketball. They were all amazed and excited to know their dear friend had been a superstar.

As the unbelievable weekend came to an end, I was sad to think about leaving this group. I had a gut feeling they would never be together again.

Maynard's 1956 state championship team honored

Twelve members of Maynard's 1956 state championship team - Coach Mel Kupferschmid, cheerleader Deanna Franklin Oppenheimer, Glenda Nicholson Thielbert, Carolyn Nicholson Borland, Dorothy Fettkether Wenger, chaperone Irene Harrington, Marlene Becker Heller, Lois Arthur Eggerth, cheerleader Jean Meyer Knoploh, Mary Anne Roquet Iliff, Barbara Fish Kalm, Janice Hoehne Steinbronn. The team was honored Saturday night in Des Moines.

Right- Maynard Hall-of-Fame sisters Glenda and Carolyn Nicholson.

Photo courtesy of The Fayette Leader

As my mom was introduced, she was on the big screen.

A picture of my mom moments after I found out she scored 3,079 points in high school.

The last time Mom would visit the farm she loved.

It was a special moment for me to see my mom and dad walking down the aisle as they did in 1957.

Me and my mom at center court in the old Maynard gym.

## CHAPTER 19
## A TOUR FULL OF GOLDEN MEMORIES

On a February day in 2009, my mom went to the doctor because she saw a flash in her eye. Her doctor was on vacation, and the doctor on call said he didn't think it was a big deal, but he called for an x-ray just to be sure.

Two days later, my mom told me with tears in her eyes that she had lung cancer and that it was serious. After further tests the next day, we got the really bad news: the cancer was stage IV and inoperable. The tumor was the size of a softball, and she was to start the ugly process of chemotherapy. My mom was scared throughout this entire process but never showed it to anyone. Deep down inside she knew what she was up against, the toughest opponent in her life. At some point she realized even though she beat the competition most of her life, she knew that this was one opponent she could not overcome.

After several rough months of chemotherapy, with the size of the tumor changing occasionally but never disappearing, we all knew my mom would not be cured. She knew she was dying.

One of Mom's last wishes was to go back to Maynard and visit the farmhouse where she grew up and also see her brother Jim and her sister Betty, who were in an assisted living facility. On September 22, 2009, Dad, my sister Liz and I drove my Mom from Madison to Maynard. Mom slept most of the way.

We stopped in Oelwein and visited Zion Lutheran Church where, a half century earlier, Mom and Dad were married. We walked into the beautiful church, and Mom and Dad walked down the aisle hand in hand, and thought about that special day so long ago.

We proceeded to Dad's childhood house, the place with the nine car garage. The tiny old house was still there, but the garage was gone. I asked my dad what had happened to the garage. He said, "In 1968 a killer tornado swept through Oelwein and Maynard. It completely destroyed the garage and left my house untouched." The current owners invited us in and gave us a tour, we couldn't believe how small Glenn's childhood home was.

Then it was on to the assisted living complex where my mom visited with Jim and Betty. Betty was very sick, and Jim was confined to a wheelchair in a separate room. Mom spent time with both of them and was very concerned about their health and comfort. Then she said her last goodbyes to her brother and sister.

We stopped at my Uncle Jim's house, and his wife Janice made a grand meal for us.

Then we went to the old Nicholson family farm outside of Maynard. As we pulled up, we saw a huge new house being built right next to the old farmhouse. It was obvious that the new owners were going to tear down Mom's childhood home.

Mom was exhausted, so we turned around and headed for home. But after we had gone a few miles I persuaded everybody that since we came that far we should go back and spend some time there.

This time when we pulled up, the owners, a friendly middle-aged couple, were outside. I explained who we were. The woman knew all about Carolyn and the Nicholsons, as her family had bought the farm from Mom's brother Jim.

We spent about thirty minutes touring the house and taking pictures. The owner of the house suggested that we take a tour of the Maynard gym, so we decided to do that, too.

When we got to the school, Mom could barely walk. The high school principal, Susan Kinneman, met us at the door and asked, "Are you Carolyn Nicholson? We have been waiting for you." The farmhouse owner had phoned Susan and told her that basketball legend Carolyn Nicholson was on the way.

Susan escorted us to the school's brand new gym. I then asked, "What happened to the old gym?"

"Oh, that's downstairs," Susan said. "We use it as a weight room."

We went downstairs and beheld the old Maynard gym, just as Mom had left it fifty-five years ago. We were amazed at how small it was.

My mom's eyes lit up as we walked onto the gym floor. She immediately recalled all the great memories that happened

in this gym more than 50 years ago. She said it seemed like yesterday. She told me. "Some of the best memories of my life happened in this gym." She looked up in the balcony recalling that
her mom and dad would always sit right there as she pointed to
the front row of the balcony. She still says she doesn't know how
they fit all the fans in the small gym. "This gym was always so
packed." Liz and I could see how proud she was to show her kids
where she played and where she became a star. We sat down
in the middle of the floor and the next thing we knew a couple
current players surrounded her as did some of the faculty as the
word spread that Carolyn Nicholson was back in the Maynard
gym.

They all wanted to meet the Maynard player, the legend
who was credited for changing girls' 6 on 6 basketball forever.
We took lots of pictures and listened to several stories of her
playing days in that gym. It was twenty minutes with my mom
in that gym that I will never forget.

As we were leaving, Susan asked, "Have you seen the
Maynard trophy case?"

I said I had not, so Susan led us down the hallway, and
there it was, the 1956 state championship trophy. That was
the first time Mom had seen the trophy since she held it on the
court in Des Moines a lifetime ago.

Then I looked on the wall and noticed a huge plaque that
listed Maynard's all-time leading scorers. The principal looked
at me and said, "Your mom is on there." And, indeed, she was
– in the third spot. The plaque said, "Carolyn Nicholson, 3,079
points."

As I stood in disbelief, I tried to calculate how many
points that was per game. I guessed that if she played for four
years it was around 30 points a game. I suggested that number
to Mom. She looked at me and simply said, "I made the team as
an eighth grader."

I hugged her and asked her, "Why didn't you tell us that
you scored 3,079 points in high school?"

She responded, "It was no big deal."

That was typical of my mom. Carolyn enjoyed life.
Among her many interests were bowling, playing bridge and

euchre, golf, following Wisconsin Badger men's basketball, and cooking. She also had a remarkable talent for making beautiful pine cone wreaths. One thing she didn't do was talk about her remarkable basketball accomplishments.

Not long after the Iowa trip, Mom got very weak and went into hospice, where she would spend her last days. On November 18, 2009, at age 72, she died.

My dad will always remember Carolyn as the World's Greatest Wife. My brother, my sister, and I will always remember her as the World's Greatest Mother.

But there are thousands of people in Iowa and elsewhere who remember Carolyn Nicholson as a 6 on 6 basketball star, a blond streak who would start at the top of the key, pump fake, dribble twice, and score, and score, and score, and score, and score....

In Memory Of
*Carolyn F. Borland*
*September 18, 1937 - November 18, 2009*

Brianna and Brooke made this potholder for you!

i Hope your cancer Gets Smaller!
From: Brooke

Dear Grandma,
I love you so much, and I always will.
Your the best grandma I have ever had!
I really hope that your cancer shrinks
and you can stop taking chemo!
Your the best grandma ever
I pray for you every day that your cancer
will shrink & keep shrinking.
I ♡ you!!!!!!thank you for always being
there for me!
Brianna p.s. I hope you will like me & Brooke present

Praying for Carolyn Nicholson Borland.

## ABOUT THE AUTHOR

Brian Borland was inspired to write this story after visiting his family's ancestral home of Maynard, Iowa, while attending his Grandmother Ruth's funeral in 2004. He realized that he might never visit that place, which had been such a vital part of his childhood, again.

In the process of writing his family's story, Brian uncovered the fascinating past of his parents – two incredible athletes with amazing accomplishments. Brian discovered that his mother Carolyn, completely unbeknownst to him, changed the face of girls' basketball in Iowa forever with her quick first step, dead-eye shot and fiery personality.

As his mother fell ill in 2009, Brian's urgency to continue his work increased. He visited the scenes of many of his parents' triumphs and heard their stories – many of which are shared in the book Maynard 8 Miles. Carolyn passed away before the publication of this book but the experience of learning her story has helped her live more vividly in his memory.

Brian is 50 years old and resides in Madison, Wisconsin, with his wife Char and 3 children: Brianna, Alex and Brooke. He lives 15 minutes from his father Glenn, for whom this truly incredible story is "no big deal."

Brian is a first time author, an IT entrepreneur and a former collegiate athlete with a passion for family, teaching and coaching. He received his BA from the University of Wisconsin-Eau Claire, where he also played Division III NCAA baseball.

# RESOURCES USED

- Associated Press.
- Beran, Janice A. From Six-on-Six to Full Court Press: A Century of Iowa Girls' Basketball
- 1993 Iowa State University Press, Ames, Iowa 50014
- The Bulletin Journal
- Capital Times Madison, WI
- Cedar Rapids Gazette
- Davenport High School Blackhawk. 1908. Davenport, IA
- Des Moines Register
- Des Moines Tribune
- Dubuque Telegraph Herald.
- Iowa Girl's High School Athletic Union. 1956 Basketball Yearbook. 11th Annual Edition
- McElwain, Max. The Only Dance in Iowa: A History of Six-player Girls' Basketball
- 2004 University of Nebraska Press, Lincoln and London
- Milwaukee Journal
- Milwaukee Sentinel
- More than a Game 6 on 6 Basketball in Iowa. Iowa Public Television Documentary Video
- Oelwein Daily Register
- Palimpsest. Iowa City, Iowa: The State Historical Society of Iowa, 1968. Edited by William J. Petersen. Issued April 1968 Volume XLIX  No.4
- Sports Illustrated
- Waterloo Courier
- Wisconsin State Journal
- Iowa Salutes the Iowa Girl-72 Years of Iowa Girls Basketball Tournaments. Fletcher Communications, 1990 Video